Michael Eldred on the Digital Age

Challenges for Today's Thinking

Interview with
M.G. Michael & Katina Michael

Cover painting: Anna Ninck *Untitled* 1993 acrylic, plastic foil on paper
41.5 x 29.5 cm

Published by M&K Press
Wollongong, NSW, Australia

ISBN 978-1-74128-338-9 (paperback)
ISBN 978-1-74128-339-6 (e-book)

Dedication

Dedicated to a more questioning mind for a more challenging world.

Contents

Preface

For some years we have been at the crossroads with our connection to modern and innovative technologies which have increasingly touched upon questions of a literal joining together of human and machine. This has led to many high-level debates and publications from experts in various disciplines from both the scientific and humanities communities. These exchanges range from discussions related to the limits (or not) of scientific progress; autonomy from technological innovations; and the pros and cons of the much-hyped singularity, the point at which technological growth becomes irreversible. From the humanities sector the questions raised have to do predominately with the ethics and morality of these scientific movements and the study of the social implications once these innovative technologies diffuse throughout society. We are fortunate that during these especially critical times for our world we are not bereft of eminently qualified and deeply reflective thinkers. Scientists and philosophers alike are keenly absorbed in this serious challenge to arrive at some sort of equilibrium before things do indeed become irreversible. We are very happy to be able to present here one of these distinguished thinkers who will describe the critical issues in this debate that directly relate to the human condition by way of the essentials of human existence. He will also deconstruct down to the semiotic level how the meaning of these discussions is communicated to us.

Our present author Michael Eldred is one of these philosophers whose voice needs to be heard as did the voices of Norbert Wiener, Lewis Mumford, Jacques Ellul and Ivan Illich decades before him. He thoroughly understands the importance of the building blocks of science and the distinction between the rational and the irrational. He had been awarded two science degrees majoring in mathematics before he immersed himself in philosophy, beginning with a doctorate where he extended the form-analytic theory of capitalist society with particular reference to Marx and Hegel. He is on solid ground with both the hard sciences and philosophy. Importantly, Eldred belongs to that notable group of scholars who fathom that a sharp dichotomy in disciplines not only prevents and does damage to the genuine cross-disciplinary discussion especially necessary nowadays, but who also knows why the liberal arts still matter. In the ancient world, rhetoric and logic were as vital to the building of knowledge as were arithmetic and geometry. These thinkers recognize that if the hard sciences get apparently far ahead of the humanities, we leave ourselves open to dangers both known and unknown. Given the escalating ubiquity of modern technological innovations, which more and more hold us tightly in their grip to mesmerize with their Utopian promises, the implications of an unchecked technological trajectory and the resultant function creep become matters that must concern us all.

We have to care about the world we live in. We have to care about the world we are leaving behind. It is an inheritance and cannot be ill-treated. People matter. Place matters. The connection between people matters. And the connection between people and place matters. We are not a throw-away society like the computers and high-tech gadgetry we build with their prearranged obsolescence. Things that inherently matter and are ultimately possessed of real value are not mass-produced on demand nor downloaded from our laptops. Nor are they, once they have been exploited, dumped in the illegal landfills of developing nations. As a community of concerned scholars, we challenge the 'move fast and break things' mentality of our generation. And here we do not mean younger people, many of whom hold grave concerns for the state of play they have been thrust into, but rather those who have put this way forward to serve their own ravenous self-interests. This is no way to live and breathe for those who do not have access to clean air and drinking water and feel they must spend what little disposable income they possess on access to the digital world — in the hope they will enter the global economy and strike it rich as well. That is no way to preserve the wondrous physical environment around us, nor the age-old practices and oral traditions that have been passed down from one generation to the next with all of its acquired wisdom. These are the ageless links that bind communities together and which have been devalued by such things as the gig economy and the rise of the corporate mentality. We have been fed lies about what is truly important in life. We have in one way or another believed in these lies and shifted both our attention and gaze to the shiny technologies that we hold in our hands or to the screens that are now more and more in front of our eyes. In some way we need to break with this vast delusion. But first, we have to discern this silver screen for what it is: a kind of deeper than 'deep fake'. It is an artificial existence driven by data and binary digits. It is a cheap and fabricated imitation. Fabricated and not comparable to the 'real thing', the person who is possessed of understanding and cognizant of her or his own existence. Important, too, is the effort of co-ordination, technology as process and not merely as product. This means empowerment of people themselves in all of their abundant humanity. We don't want to be defined by *whatness* as Eldred in many places points out. Because we are *who* we are as humans. We are not empty vessels or mere subjects or mere objects. And human beings are obviously different from machines which are pure apparatuses made up of cogs and wheels and circuitry. Humans are capable of compassion and empathy; they can practise forgiveness and are able to perform charity. They perspire and bleed. Each life brought into this world is unique. Importantly, machines do not understand existential risk in the context of their own existence.

The strength, we could even say, the beauty of Eldred's thought is that it is brave in taking on the received mantra that today's ever-progressing technoscience, with its mathematical and empirical methods, captures the deepest truths of the world, rather than representing the absolute will to control and manipulate its movements. He is not afraid of clearing away the debris of our entrenched and oftentimes thoughtless preconceptions or of upsetting the status quo of the current predominant mind-set that shapes our world; the great reset, as it has often been described in recent times. Eldred gets as close as possible to the simplest, most elementary phenomena, in order to interpret them as plainly as possible. He succeeds as a hermeneutic phenomenologist in finding the middle path between the two great warring modern expressions of philosophy, the analytic (Bertrand Russell, G. E. Moore, Ludwig Wittgenstein, Karl Popper) and the continental (Hegel, Nietzsche, Foucault, Deleuze) traditions.

Eldred gives us a view of the machine. Not the machine in terms of the *computational thing*, that is, the artefact, the device but the *machine* behind the machine, the system or set of correlated principles in our mind and how it operates. Eldred speaks of stakeholders and interplay and the gainful game, and demystifies the process of manipulation (and/or being) in its plainest, most elegant form. How does this system actually work? Who are the stakeholders? How do technology magnates make it happen? Why do we follow and revere the present-day memes as truth? What are the mental models that form in our minds and why have we succumbed to this propaganda? What is the greatest disinformation and who is mastering the puppet and to what ends? Especially in this internet-fuelled world where one of the greatest resources of our time has been usurped by commercial interests. Why will humankind continually succumb to greed when there are other modes of existence that would serve us much better? Perhaps it is on account of the 'hungry ghost' of avarice, and an aversion to the prospect of death. And certainly because of *currency*, that is, money, which neither listens nor hears but gobbles up and mows down anything and everything in its path.

The techno-myth has prevailed as have secular ideologies that seem to have taken us away from the very essence of feeling something innately, inwardly, inside ourselves, in our heart, the centre of our spiritual activity. Our 'heart' as a bodily organ is physically inside, but, in Eldred's thinking, the heart is in truth the pulsating resonance with the encompassing whole that we all share with one another. Doing is not necessarily feeling. Keeping busy behind the screen of a machine is not necessarily acting to develop what matters in the world: discovery, curiosity, and human connection. The machines we have created have not come equipped with a resonating heart, despite the personification of the computer's central processing unit (CPU) as heart. If we are heart-less, it then follows we are on a path that has devalued who the other is. We see money, we don't estimate another's whoness. We see customers, we don't see people appreciatively. We seek to know of subscribers and followers, we don't seek to foster that which gives our life its joy, true and empathetic human connection in relationships.

Ontological categories such as being, existence and reality are all the time more viewed as 'files'. In this generation, we distance ourselves from one another while at the same time demanding that we do more about our mental health and well-being. Such a frightening irony. The challenge, it seems, is to recognize the 'game' for what it is and the 'machine' for what it is. The machine is not the mechanism or apparatus by which I can send an e-mail or make a mobile phone call or access Google Search. The machines are the "mechanics" behind our socio-economic and socio-political structures and institutions that need to be scrutinized and unravelled, as Jeremy Pitt from Imperial College London sagaciously presents in his work on democracy-by-design. From Eldred we can see 'the machine', presented in bare bones, for what it is, and we can discover how we might consider reshaping it, and seeking more authentic modes of communication. Ultimately, according to Eldred, the 'machine' is our shared mind-set in this digital age. This mind-set, he says, can be historically recast.

In the end, Michael Eldred is asking us one of the most important questions of the 21st century: *Why could not progress consist of taking a step back into more elementary truths than modern science and technology are ever able to uncover, and which they seem intent on covering up?*

M.G. Michael & Katina Michael,
Gerringong, NSW, Australia, April 2021

1. Technology and Consciousness

1.1. How has technology been understood down through the ages? Has the understanding of technology been received or practised differently in what we today call the Digital Age?

In today's sense, technology results from wedding modern science with a practical or industrial art. In an older sense, closer to the ancient Greek, 'technologia' is a "systematic treatment (of grammar, etc.)" (OED). The coupling of modern science with a practical application can therefore be aptly called technoscience, whose application consists in producing something efficiently. By contrast, in earlier times the art of making shoes or cloth would not have been called technology, although a treatise on the art of making shoes or cloth could have been.

I understand the Digital Age as our own times in which electronic digital technologies have emerged that enable the building of an artificial world in which digital data, or bit-strings, circulate and trigger effects under the control of algorithms — the cyberworld. The 'cyber' in cyberworld comes from the ancient Greek meaning 'to steer, to govern'.[11] The algorithms embedded in the cyberworld are the 'governors' of this artificial world, effectively, efficiently governing the movements of all the cyberworld's denizens, its binary data. The cyberworld can be thought of as a technologically enabled, artificial replication of the physical world in digitized form. Everything in the physical world has its digitized surrogate in the cyberworld, even to the extent that the surrogate usurps the physical original. As such, the cyberworld is not just an identical or non-identical digital twin of the physical world, but has the inherent tendency to substitute for it.

Just as there are many beings in the physical world, there are also many algorithms steering the cyberworld that can also come into conflict with one another in the form of digital viruses that can serve as surrogates of human actors for cyber-attacks and cyber-warfare. In this sense, automated bit-strings substitute for human beings. The automated, algorithmic outsourcing of our understanding and control of movements in the world to the cyberworld that also enables the viral infection of bit-strings is a momentous, unparalleled world-historical event, by subverting, once and for all, the venerable paradigm of efficient, productive movement that is the hallmark of all Western science: automated movement controlled by a single source

---

1 The term 'cybernetics' was coined by Norbert Wiener in 1948 as "the scientific study of control and communication in the animal and the machine". *Cybernetics: Or Control and Communication in the Animal and the Machine* Cambridge, Massachusetts, MIT Press 1948. The term 'cyberworld' goes beyond this definition to encompass the social world as steered and controlled by algorithms.

can now be countermanded and outsmarted by another, adversarial, automated source. Power interplay can henceforth be played out automatically via opposing bit-strings.

On a deeper level, the cyberworld is not just an artificially constructed network inhabited by bit-strings comprising algorithms and data, but also a mind-set in which we all partake as the latest iteration of a mathematized mode of accessing and controlling the world's movements. The key to understanding the cyberworld is to conceive it as both the mind-set and the artificial realization of the algorithmized, automated control of all kinds of movement. More on this topic of the will to power later on.

1.2. What is technique? Is it important to have some knowledge of what technique actually means and the origins of the word itself? And why?

The word 'technique' entered English from the French which, in turn, is adopted from the German 'Technik' that is a synonym for 'technology' or 'engineering' in the sense of applied science, i.e. technoscience. But 'technique' in English has broader and more subtle connotations of the 'art' of doing something that may not even produce any end-product. Thus we have, even with the ancient Greeks, the art of making money, the art of rhetoric, the art of playing a musical instrument, the art of lovemaking, and so on. When I play the guitar, I have a certain technique that allows me to make music that is in the playing itself and does not result in a separate end-product. For the Greeks, this is a *praxis*, i.e. a movement or energy that contains its end within itself. If, however, I make a recording of my playing, this is a movement of production that requires modern electronic recording technology, which is merely a tool to capture my individual technique of playing. Technoscience, by contrast, is the application of general scientific laws to a particular application that, in turn, should be distinguished from a singular technique of playing that is my very own. Technoscience transforms the art of making something into a production process governed in line with physical laws. The machines in the production process are today invariably controlled by digital algorithms to a lesser or greater extent, thus automating their functioning.

The Greek word for an art is τέχνη (technae). Thus Plato speaks of many different techniques or arts such as the art of persuasion, the art of flattery, the art of household management, the art of hunting, etc. But when it comes to asking what movement is, Plato fixes his gaze on the paradigm of specifically productive art, i.e. τέχνη ποιητική (technae poiaetikae), such as the carpenter's art of making a table. Plato performs this restriction in the sense of τέχνη not for the sake of understanding τέχνη itself but for understanding what movement and change are as modes of being. Aristotle follows Plato's lead by taking productive technique as the paradigm for fashioning his own ontology of movement with its famous triple of concepts: potential, energy and entelechy (finished presence). The Greek words for movement in this broad sense are κίνησις (kinaesis, as in our modern sense of kinetic energy) and μεταβολή (metabolae, as in our English word 'metabolism'), meaning 'change', 'turnover' or 'transformation,' but also 'interchange' and 'exchange' as in an exchange of views in a rhetorical situation or the exchange of goods on the market.

The entire phenomenality of movement, change and becoming was at the heart of the questions posed by incipient Greek philosophy. Plato makes the crucial distinction between becoming (γένεσις, genesis) and being in his dialogue, *Timaios*. There he distinguishes genesis, as one fundamental kind of movement or change (becoming), from being as that which is everlastingly unchanging (ἀεὶ ὄν, aei on), thus providing only a negative determination of being as the negation of genesis, i.e. as non-movement The question lying behind this remains: how is being itself to be understood positively in its own right as distinct from becoming, movement, change. For Plato it is inadmissible to simply declare, as the Heracliteans did, that all is in flux, for there are for him also the unchanging ideas, or literally, 'sights' and 'looks,' of what things are. For example, the carpenter has the unchanging idea or sight of a table mentally in view as the end-point of his productive movement when setting about making a table. On the basis of his productive know-how, he envisages a table in advance as the idea that guides his productive activity. Again it is important to underscore that productive technique per se is not the focus of interest, but is the paradigm employed to make the phenomena of movement and being clearer ontologically, that is, as modes of being. It is a fateful decision of philosophical questioning at that time to restrict the understanding of τέχνη (technae) to τέχνη ποίητική (technae poiaetikae), a decision with consequences down through the ages up to and including our modern age of technoscience.

Martin Heidegger takes up his radical question concerning the meaning of being itself (der Sinn des Seins), as distinct from the traditional metaphysical question concerning the meaning of the being of beings, i.e. their beingness. In doing so, he repeats the same fateful truncation as Plato did in taking productive technique as the paradigm for all kinds of movement without so much as mentioning that the Greek understanding of technique encompasses many different arts besides the productive ones. This truncation amounts to a narrowing of philosophical vision to a kind of tunnel vision. Why? Plato and Aristotle were fixated on the paradigm of productive movement in tackling the phenomenon of movement with a view to master it knowingly.

A recast ontology of movement must consider those kinds of movement and change that are interchanges and interplay among multiple players rather than the production of something proceeding from a single governing source or ἀρχή (archae). Such interplay is unpredictable, incalculable. For traditional metaphysics, starting with Plato and Aristotle, unpredictability was anathema, and Aristotle explicitly excluded contingency, that is, that which just comes along (κατὰ συμβεβηκός), from investigation in his *Metaphysics*. A pivotal example of interplay is the art of rhetoric, which Aristotle tried to press into his productive ontology of movement. In doing so, he does violence to the phenomenon of the rhetorical situation as fundamentally an interchange and interplay of views and opinions among a plurality of players, rather than the well-aimed production of a certain mood in the trustful audience by a skilful orator. Heidegger misses the opportunity of attempting an ontology of interplay as a kind of movement sui generis. This would have been as radical a departure from the traditional metaphysical posing of the question concerning the being of beings employing the productive paradigm as is Heidegger's own question concerning the meaning of being itself. Instead of conceiving being simply as non-movement, as Plato and Aristotle implicitly did, Heidegger uncovers that the meaning of being itself is implicitly *temporal*, a finding with enormous implications, to which I shall return.

1.3. How have others conceived technology and technique?

Others approaching the question concerning technology and technique, including the Frankfurt school old and new, have not had ontological questions in mind at all. When asking what technology is, the focus must be on technology as a mode of being fixated on productive movement. For instance, the conception of "instrumental reason" in Adorno and Horkheimer, and adopted by many others influenced by so-called Critical Theory, does not live up to being an ontological concept fashioned to capture what movement is as a mode of being. Adorno, in particular, set up a hostile opposition between dialectics in the Hegelian sense and ontology. The latter, now transformed by Heidegger into the question concerning the meaning of being itself, was considered by Adorno in his *Negative Dialektik* as a "disgusting term" (dégoutanter Terminus). The irony of Adorno's championing dialectics over ontology is that Hegel's dialectical thinking in his *Logik* is precisely what Hegel himself expressly calls his ontology. With Adorno's pronouncement, an entire generation of the (West) German left was discouraged from questoning ontologically altogether. Although Adorno championed dialectics over positivism, his distaste for ontology has had the effect of closing off the ontological difference just as effectively as positivism has done.

To come to grips with the phenomenality of modern technoscience in all its guises, ranging through both the physical and social sciences, requires conceiving productive technique in the Greek sense as the germ for *gaining mastery* over movement and change of all kinds. Kurzweil, for instance, may be regarded as an extreme proponent of total control over movement, including especially that movement of mortal human beings toward death. Bill & Melinda Gates' focus on eradicating diseases that have long since plagued humankind is another example of technoscientific thinking. The ancient Greeks found solace in the celestial phenomenon of the everlasting periodic movement of the fixed stars around the Earth that was reliable and eternally the same, although it is nonetheless movement. This eternal recurrence of the stars in their motion relieved their anxiety that the world could vanish, and was taken by Plato as an image for the eternal, unmoving ideas that constituted, at least, the supposedly unchanging, everlasting ontological structure of the world. Other cultures, too, have gazed at the 'everlasting' circling of the stars and developed their own cosmological and religious ideas, but they have not concerned themselves with explicit ontological questions.

Today the question remains as to how to come to terms with those sociating movements that are interchanges and interplays among two or many players, not with the prefixed aim of gaining control over them through some kind of predictive or precalculating knowledge. Rather, the aim must be to understand them simply as the phenomena that they show themselves to be to our mind, in order to adopt an appropriate attitude toward them. In particular, insight into phenomena of interplay goes hand in hand with an acceptance of the uncertainty of interplayful movements and a renunciation of trying to get them within a controlling grasp. Instead of mastery and control, mutual esteem and estimation as well as negotiation are called for, as I shall elaborate further.

This has implications also for understanding human relations with today's digitized machines, namely, as interplay. These machines of all kinds, whether it be a smart phone or a printing press, are steered automatically by algorithms, and these algorithms are written by human beings, even when the algorithms 'learn' via artificial neural networks. Control over human life-movements themselves increasingly becomes algorithmically mediated. The machines themselves are implanted with countless myriads of Universal Turing Machines, i.e. algorithms, that churn through the digital data fed into them. What a user of a particular digital machine or network of machines, such as the internet, can or cannot do is dictated by the algorithms which can be more or less authoritarian, more or less dialogical. The former corresponds to strict control over movement and thus to the paradigm of mastery of movement from a governing source. The latter, on the other hand, corresponds to the paradigm of interchange, whereby the algorithm itself modifies its behaviour according to the user's responses rather than dictating what the user must do.

1.4. How do you understand consciousness? How does it differ from intelligence? How does it differ from psyche?

The question concerning consciousness is weighty. In the first place I understand consciousness as the concept substituting for the original Greek concept of psyche, often rendered as 'soul' in English. In Cartesian metaphysics and thereafter, through Kant to Husserl, consciousness is that site inside the human subject where all sorts of representations of the external world, mediated by the senses, can appear. If, like the psyche, consciousness is not a being but a mode of being, it makes no sense to locate it anywhere at all, let alone 'inside' the subject. Be that as it may, the representations inside consciousness must be understood in the very broad sense, starting with sensations that can be worked up into representations of certain objects in the external world via-à-vis the subject. Intelligence in this context is the faculty of understanding[2] that is

2 The faculty of understanding (Verstand) is introduced by Kant in contradistinction to reason (Vernunft) in his famous *Critique of Pure Reason*. Understanding (or intelligence) is that faculty of the soul (Gemüt) that is tasked with mastering (the movements of) natural entities conceived as objects (Gegenstände).

able to collect and organize the multiplicity of sensations received into representations of objects according to certain logical rules. This collecting of sensuous intuitions into categories of understanding is what constitutes them within subjectivity as objects. Hence the objectivity of objects, i.e. the very idea of an object, is an ontological achievement of the subject's inner subjectivity with the aid of transcendental, i.e. a priori, categorial intelligence. For Kant, beyond understanding, which is anchored in empirical experience, lies the realm of reason that takes flight from the ground of empirical experience and is therefore, for Kant, 'flighty'. Reason is then given a role for formulating ideals and imperatives that for Kant is the domain of practical reason, i.e. morality.

Decisive in the ontological casting of objectivity in subjectivist metaphysics is that subjective consciousness is encapsulated inside, isolated from both the external world and other similarly encapsulated subjective consciousnesses. Its lines of communication with the outside are exclusively via the sense organs in the present. Hence it becomes an ontological problem how such mutually isolated consciousnesses could be collected in some way into some kind of collective consciousness or so-called intersubjectivity. This is attempted, for instance, via the 'collective intentionality of will,' although the sense of intentionality remains hazy. The second option for conceiving intersubjectivity is language as medium of communication among subjects. Hence the sustained and dominating interest in the philosophy of language in the twentieth century among philosophers of subjectivity, which comprises pretty much all philosophers. But what is language, i.e. what is the λόγος, the logos? To countenance the possibility that there is a prelinguistic logos (from Gk. λέγειν, legein, 'to say, to glean, to gather') that gathers what presents itself in the world in a prelinguistic understanding within three-dimensional time (see below) already eludes the problematic of conventional language philosophy in which language is taken as an empirical given. We do not share the world because we communicate via language, but rather, we have language because we always already share the openness of the world and, more deeply, the openness of three-dimensional time. Language is enabled (not caused) by 3D-time.

The real problem for any ontological concept of intersubjectivity, however, lies in enclosing consciousness inside a subject in the first place, a problem with which mainstream (or academic) philosophy yet has come to grips or even acknowledge as a problem. Consciousness is taken by academic philosophy as a given, experiential *fact* (which is correct). When asked, however, what the (ontological) *truth* of consciousness is (which is to be sited in 3D-temporality, as we shall see), academic philosophy has scant little to say. The conception of an isolated, enclosed consciousness is nevertheless a perfect fit for conceiving an intelligent digital machine that can be equipped internally with automated algorithmic intelligence as a stand-alone unit. Hence it becomes easy to treat algorithmically controlled machines ontologically on a par with human beings. A machine and a conscious subject are both kinds of whats in the ontology of subjectivity, and machines can even slip conveniently into the status of subject in this ontology. That is, they ostensibly share the same mode of being as sub-jective, under-lying. For human beings, conscience and morality, for instance, then become a mere add-on, a part of the ethical superstructure rather than being implicated already in an ontology of estimative interplay.

The Greek conception of the human psyche, in contrast to consciousness, was never saddled with this problem of an inside-outside split. It is broader, more encompassing. Moreover, what today are the objects of subjective consciousness were the under-lying subjects, i.e. ὑποκείμενα (hypokeimena), for Greek thinking. These subjects were addressed by the categories (κατηγορίαι) and thus spoken about *as* such-and-such. One could say that our Western mind has been turned topsy-turvy over the millennia which, however, does not prevent translators from the ancient Greek into English speaking insensitively of beings (ὄντα , onta) as 'objects'. Descartes' pronouncement, cogito ergo sum, cast and postulated the 'I am' as the underlying subject to be the master of all the objects in the external world that were to be controlled by an interrogating consciousness demanding certain truth as to their movements. Such a positing of the subject as the final, underlying instance is foreign to ancient Greek thinking, but it was this metaphysical positing that fired the modern scientific age from the outset.

Today it is taken for granted that the human being is a conscious subject that (not who) underlies (sub-jectum), at least in principle, all movements in the world by virtue of having calculable foreknowledge of them and, in many cases, being able to control them through appropriate technologies. The cyberworld is the latest iteration and perhaps the culmination of this will to power over movement that germinated already with the ancient Greeks. Ironically, however, as is quickly becoming apparent in recent decades, the outsourcing of our piecewise understanding of the world into automatically operating algorithms uploaded to the cyberworld has turned the tables on us humans, who are supposed to be the underlying subjects, turning us instead into algorithmically surveillable objects. This development has been pin-pointed as one major source of the so-called crisis in liberal democracies, with many calling for 'us' to 'regain control'. This is a futile call because, from the outset, liberal democracy was conceived on the misguided preconception of a collective subjectivity. Such subjectivity was already undermined by the emergence of the gainful game called capitalism played in the medium of thingified value, as we shall see below.

1.5. Is it possible for an advanced digital technology to ever possess consciousness?

A key feature of the term 'consciousness' ('conscience' in French), of which Descartes makes explicit note, is that it means literally 'co-knowing. This co-knowing is at the heart of what we understand by conscience in the moral sense and it is also the reason why all consciousness is self-consciousness, i.e. consciousness can reflect, or literally, bend back upon itself in observing itself. Hence, from the start, there is a doubling of consciousness into consciousness and reflective self-consciousness, and thus a conception of an inner self, a conscience that is constantly looking over your shoulder.

Is it possible for advanced technology, by which we mean today algorithmically driven, digital technology, to achieve such a feat of doubling itself in self-reflection? What could be the analogue of a self of self-consciousness in digital technology? The analogue of representations must be the digital data representing objects 'out there' in the external world. These digital data, which are nothing other than bit-strings, are worked upon stepwise by digital intelligence, namely the algorithms, which are themselves nothing other than bit-strings, to produce a third bit-string as output, which may be another representation of, say, an image, or simply an on or off command for a certain device, or an input into a further algorithm, or the answer to a question, etc. There is nothing in the Universal Turing Machine, which is conceptually the elementary core for all possible computers (at least up to quantum computers, which modifies the conception), and therefore quasi the ontological blueprint for the cyberworld, corresponding to a reflective self: Further algorithmic calculations of a given output do not amount to a bending-back on itself but simply to a continuation of algorithmic processing. The scanning head of a Universal Turing Machine 'sees' (detects via an electromagnetic signal) only one binary digit, or bit, at a time in its sequential algorithmic steps, and even a quantum computer 'sees' only an ambiguity of one or zero at each discrete step. Parallel computing, too, does not amount to a bending-back of the computation onto itself, but only to several step-calculations being executed in parallel. The computer processes its algorithms but does not observe itself 'conscientiously' doing this processing. In other words, it has no self and does not know what it is doing.

There is a further, deeper hurdle for an algorithmically driven digital device artificially emulating human consciousness that resides in the conception of subjective consciousness itself. This hindrance lies in the tripartite Kantian conception of transcendental subjectivity consisting of pure sensuous intuition, pure categorial understanding and their connecting, synthesizing link, namely, the pure power of imagination. The power of imagination is able to gather the multiplicity of sensuous representations in the three dimensions of apprehension, reproduction and recognition that can be plausibly interpreted, as Heidegger does in detail, as three, independent, and thus non-linear, temporal dimensions of present, fast and future. With this phenomenological reinterpretation of consciousness as immersion in three-dimensional time, leave is finally taken from the entrenched conception of human being as subjective consciousness, and the ontological gulf between subjective consciousness and any conceivable digital device becomes even vaster, for the latter lacks anything remotely resembling this temporally reinterpreted power of imagination.

Any algorithmically driven device at all sequentially works through algorithms step-by-step. A Turing machine's scanning head can only detect, via an electromagnetic signal, the bit it is currently scanning in the present; it is open neither to past nor future nor, strictly speaking, even to the present (which only *we* can perceive, not the scanning head itself). This holds true also of parallel processing, which is merely a parallel running of several sequential processings, and even of quantum computers whose qubits (quantum binary digits) assume (ambiguous) states sequentially. Of course, I am aware that this remark about the three-dimensional temporal nature of human consciousness, or better, of the human psyche, initially must remain cryptic, for it requires a long and slow discursive path to gain such an insight. It is hard to take leave of the conception of linear time that is so intimately fused with efficient causality.[3] In the following, I shall briefly say something more on the human psyche as three-dimensional time.

3 Such leave-taking does not amount merely to Humean scepticism. Rather, it is required by an alternative ontology of movement as interplay which cannot be properly conceived within the strictures of one-dimensional, efficient-causal time.

2. Artificial Intelligence and Mind

2.1. Can a machine ever become spiritual?

As to whether a machine could be spiritual, i.e. related to spirit, I take the word here, on the one hand, as a synonym for German 'Geist' which, in turn, is a synonym for Greek νοῦς (nous). Nous is that faculty of the human psyche which is able to understand the world, i.e. its intellect or mind, by seeing the eidetic 'looks' of beings. On the other hand, 'spirit' is a standard translation of Greek πνεῦμα (pneuma), the 'breath' or 'animating principle' in living beings. Hence it is a synonym for ψυχή (psychae), 'anima', 'soul'. The human psyche itself is not a being of any kind but, as I recast it, the mode of being of human being itself, as open to the world and existing in it with others. Nous enables human beings to understand what comes to presence (presence) or goes into absence (absence) within the openness that I am here calling the psyche. The psyche, can be identified with the *openness of three-dimensional time* itself in which everything possible occurs, presencing and absencing, perhaps haphazardly, for the mind. Under the power of imagination, the mind can move freely through all three temporal dimensions, not necessarily in any linear fashion. For anything at all to 'be', it must presence in the psyche's open three-dimensional time in one way or the other. We human beings always understand the world in some way or other, even if it is a misunderstanding. This implies that occurrences can come to presence, i.e. occur, for the mind also in deceptive and misleading ways, but such deceptive occurrences are not simply non-existent. Even deceptions and obfuscations must come to presence for the mind. Hence the question of truth (revealing and concealing) must not be confused with the question of being (presencing and absencing). Being itself has a temporal meaning as presencing or absencing in three-dimensional time. Whether such presencing or absencing for the psychic mind is deceptive, obfuscating or concealing is another related, but separate question.

We humans can also *articulate* an understanding of the world in language, i.e. in the λόγος (logos). Such understanding in terms of λόγος is essentially discrete due to the nature of articulated language itself and is thus reducible to a countable string of syllables, characters, letters, that in principle may be infinitely, albeit countably, long, which in turn can be digitized in binary code encapsulating this understanding as a digital algorithm. The algorithm is thus the binary representation of the human understanding of some practical situation, such as placing an order online. This algorithm derived by coding our human understanding of a practical situation, when inserted into a computing device of some kind as a bit-string, can then be fed with digital data to control some movement or other. The algorithm itself has no understanding of the world nor any psychic openness to three-dimensional time. The digital data themselves are gathered with the aid of algorithms that register movements in the cyberworld. These movements may stem from physical movements (e.g. weather) or from human users who interface with the cyberworld (e.g. behaviour in a social medium). The user-data can then trigger a further cybernetic movement such as sending an advertisement to the user's digital device, or something more sinister, as when the state surveills what its citizens are up to by infiltrating a Trojan virus into devices and systems.

It is always our own, human understanding of (some segment of) the world in such-and-such a way, from a given perspective, that can be transformed into an algorithm (i.e. coded, digitized), and this understanding is always an interpretation, that is, it is hermeneutic, being dependent on the fundamental interpretation of the world in a given historical time, which I term its *onto-hermeneutic cast*. The onto-hermeneutic cast provides the ontological structure or scaffolding that determines *AS what* or *AS who* beings show themselves in the world to the mind in a given age. 'Cast' is to be understood here in its threefold sense of i) a mould or form, ii) a throw, and iii) a role, as in actors being cast into their roles in a play. It is in terms of the respective onto-hermeneutic cast of an age that we understand the world from within this mind-set and can translate segments of this understanding into digital algorithms.

There are claims made these days that digital machines are beginning to learn to write their own algorithms based on 'deep learning' from mountains of data input into them, but it is we who set the limiting parameters (such as the weightings of data in multi-layered, artificial neuronal networks) for the task *in mind* and also determine which data are to be mined. Hence, e.g. recently in Bonn a computer was fed the fragment of an unfinished work by Beethoven and given the task of completing it on the basis of criteria set by the programmers and empirical data in the form of musical samples. Does this amount to an artificial mind at work? If there were an artificial equivalent to nous, Geist, mind, it would reside in the algorithms that 'understand' the data input by computing them one way or another to calculate an output. Is computing equivalent to understanding? Or are algorithms mining mountains of data simply very efficient at pattern-recognition, thus drawing 'conclusions' by reproducing *previous*, already existing patterns? Algorithms of any kind proceed step-by-step in a causal-logical way, i.e. mechanically in the sense of a Turing machine; they envisage no εἶδος (eidos) in advance, nor do they have an end (τέλος, telos) 'in mind' toward which they work to bring it to finished presence, nor do they know what they are doing in the sense of self-reflection, observing themselves. In this sense, algorithms do not even emulate the paradigm of productive technique, for which the guiding sight of an eidos is essential. Nor do algorithms possess the spontaneity of nous to which an εἶδος (eidos), i.e.an idea, can spontaneously, freely appear. It is the programmer who must envisage an idea, digitize it and implant it in a digital device. Moreover, ideas pop into the mind from any of the three temporal dimensions, often haphazardly; the mind itself is therefore temporally three-dimensional and its movements anything but linear. Neither modern science nor today's philosophy, however, know anything at all of three-dimensional time; they know only of the traditional, one-dimensional, linear time counted off movement. Even Einsteinian relativity, of which today's physics remains immensely proud, operates merely with one-dimensional, linear time measured by a clock and reduces this linear time itself to the movement of light that is postulated to be the absolute movement in both special and general relativity theory.

2.2. Is Artificial Intelligence (AI) going to rule the world one day? And, if yes, in what sense? What are some of the hidden biases in AI?

Artificial Intelligence (AI) relies on letting digital algorithms loose in the cyberworld to control all kinds of movements. Already garden-variety computers rely on gathering digital data that enable a digital representation of some practical situation in the world and its further algorithmic calculation to compute a result that can be used to master some kind of movement, e.g. a prediction, an on-off switch, the production of a digital image, a medical diagnosis, and so on. The digital algorithm, if it has been appropriately conceived and written, represents a logical understanding of some aspect of the world that, when applied in a calculation of digital data, outputs a useful result. It is the computer programmer who envisages in advance what the algorithm is supposed to do, i.e. the programmer has an idea or εἶδος (eidos) in mind from the temporal dimension of the future. Such algorithms are already deployed ubiquitously, governing what we human users of digital devices can and cannot do, enabling and thwarting our life-movements. AI in the guise of artificial neural networks and so-called deep learning through mining huge heaps of data enables even more room for the algorithms to move. For then the algorithmic steps themselves depend on thresholds being reached or not at the neural nodes which, in turn, depends on myriads of weighted data fed into a predetermined node on its specified level from various sources. The steps in the digital calculation thus become bewilderingly complicated and are no longer a programmed stepwise logical working-through of data by a given algorithm. Rather, the algorithm modifies itself according to the outputs it itself generates at predetermined nodes on various levels. The various levels are supposed to represent 'deep learning', which is merely the hyperbole of propagandists. The 'deep learning' itself depends on which learning data are fed in, thus opening the floodgates of data bias that are today well-documented. The bias itself arises because the 'deep learning' algorithm only 'learns' by recognizing patterns in existing *past* data that are then extrapolated to the future to predict, say, human behaviour in a given situation. Such 'deep learning' AI hence remains empiricist through and through, calculating only a posteriori, that is 'after the event', and never spontaneously casting a future. In this sense, AI, always and in its very conception, 'comes too late'.

There is no limit whatever ontically-factually to how AI algorithms can be deployed to control all kinds of movements that can be governed from a single source, which is the algorithm itself. Whether this control is appropriate or not is another issue depending upon how the programmers have conceived the practical situation and then encoded it. Already with a plurality of algorithms, however, a problem of principle arises that must be termed ontological. This is because the ontology of productive movement and change inherited ultimately from Aristotle (and Plato) depends on the movement emanating from a single, independent source. Where there is a plurality of sources of movement acting independently, the movement itself must be conceived as an *Interplay* defying precalculability and therefore prone to uncertainty. Because of the independence of the sources of movement, it does not suffice to attempt to master the situation via an *interaction* of reciprocal causes (since they may not react or not according to any law of reciprocal action). AI, of course, is not deterred by such a limitation in principle, nor does it even notice it. It can revert to precalculating various plausible scenarios depending on the assumed moves of the various players and then weight the various scenarios with probabilities that amount to mere guesses. This is precisely what is done in, say, war games or prognostications of economic trends that depend on making certain fixed assumptions which tie down some of the variables in the calculation, i.e. moves of the various players, to model various envisaged, possible outcome-scenarios. Such situations as economic developments or war games are in principle, i.e. ontologically, already of a different kind from complicated games such as chess or go because the rules of the latter restrict the possible moves of two opposing players to a (very large, but nevertheless) finite number that can be computed by a 'number-crunching' supercomputer. The potential moves of combatants in a war or of players on the world markets, by contrast, are infinite in number, indeed uncountably so, owing to the freedom of movement of human beings as the sources of their own life-movements and hence the unpredictability of their next move. Such moves cannot be exhaustively precalculated, but are often surprising and bewildering. The game unfolds in entirely unforeseen ways. Hence, in matters of war, commerce and politics, as well as other kinds of movements of the nature of interplay, chance is always and essentially in play.

An everyday example to see the ontological impotence of AI is its deployment in digital advertising to nudge consumers in a certain direction to purchase a certain product that a given consumer may have looked at in its digital representation (an ad). Such suggestive nudging by persuasive algorithms is basically rhetorical in the sense of an art of persuasion. The persuasiveness or not of the algorithms has to be assessed by the programmers and not by the algorithms themselves. The most famous treatise on rhetoric is Aristotle's *Art of Rhetoric* that, highly significantly, tries to press rhetoric ontologically into the mould of a productive technique like carpentry. Such ontological violence to the phenomena of interplay requiring mutual trust, estimation and esteem is perpetrated throughout the entire tradition of Western thinking in philosophy and the sciences. Western knowledge consists in foreseeing, forecasting and hence, in some sense, mastering movements, no matter whether these attempts are ontologically misguided or not. Modern philosophy since Descartes has placed epistemology, the theory of knowledge, front and centre in its endeavours, to the utter withering and neglect of any genuinely ontological considerations of how beings as such are hermeneutically cast. Knowledge in the Greek sense of ἐπιστήμη (epistaemae) was alway concerned with foreknowledge of movement. Such movements could be necessary (οὐκ ἄλλως ἔχειν or 'having it no other way'), regular (ἐπι τὸ πολύ or 'in most cases') or contingent (κατὰ συμβεβηκός or 'according to what just comes along'), whereby only the former two provide any opportunity for foreknowing.

The rise of mathematical statistics in the nineteenth century was a response to increasingly complicated physical movements, such as Brownian motion, but this branch of mathematics has become increasingly important for scientific attempts to calculate, at least probabilistically, movements/changes that defy straightforward causal calculation. For instance, medicine is heavily reliant on statistical methods to assess whether its treatments are beneficial or harmful by carrying out experiments and trials on large enough samples that provide results within statistical margins of error. This is so, even though the effects of a medication on the body are assumed, in principle, to be causal. Statistical methods become even more important for mastering situations of human interplay, such as the behaviour of people in certain situations, e.g. elections, where only *past* patterns of behaviour can be plausibly extrapolated and efficient causality becomes hazy at best. Modern psychology, too, would be at a complete loss to carry out any studies without mathematical statistical methods, which can also be incorporated into AI algorithms. In all these cases, mathematical statistical methods are useful only for large numbers of empirical observations because they can only ascertain certain general tendencies and establish regularities, but not unambiguously determine individual cases. The mathematical-statistical, empirical approach remains firmly committed to efficient causality in principle, and resorts to probabilistic calculations only because the situations under consideration are empirically complex, defying any empirical observation and measurement of individual causal interconnections.

2.3. If the movement toward an entirely efficient and autonomous AI is the goal, and if that is not altogether good, is there a way to stop this risky trajectory?

The dream of an entirely efficient and autonomous AI is a totalitarian goal that would outsource the control of our human life-movements to algorithms, thus rendering us as the pawns of these autonomously working algorithms. Such algorithms can be put into operation by corporations or technocratic governments or cyber-criminals. This dream is being sold to us today by the prophets of AI with the promise of efficiency, convenience, security and especially the promise of recovering and maintaining health, which amounts to controlling the movement of mortal human life toward death, in which we all have a stake. Such a vision of total control by algorithmically outsourcing our understanding of the world overlooks, for one thing, that these algorithms are many, from many human sources (hackers) putting them into operation, and themselves are engaged in an uncontrollable, often rivalrous and hostile interplay with one another. The movement controlled by one algorithm can be counteracted and even subverted by another algorithm infiltrating a digital virus into the first algorithm. Hence the potential for outsourcing human conflicts to conflicts among the algorithms themselves through infected algorithms, cyberattacks, cyber-warfare, etc. Even the race for cyber-security is constantly being undermined by ever more sophisticated algorithms unleashed to break encrypted code and insert algorithmic viruses to subvert the originally intended secure control of movements. Both cybercrime and state surveillance rely on such digital Trojan viruses.

The power interplay inherent in all the intertwinings of our own life-movements as players sharing a world with one another can itself be digitized into bit-strings and outsourced to the surrogate cyberworld. This applies in particular to our rivalrous interplay, which gains its digitized counterpart in the cyberworld through surrogate algorithms. Thus, for instance, the interplay of players in dialogue can be poisoned when mediated by social media algorithms that enable the interchange of nasty, hate-filled personal attacks and false information, and this socially corrosive interchange can even be outsourced to algorithmic bots.

The defence against such an escalation of the dream of total algorithmic control can only lie in human freedom itself as the source of its own free movements, in this case, of *resistance*. To resist we first have to see the danger. There can be no freedom where blindness reigns, and enlightenment about what algorithmic control over our lives is factually perpetrating in specific cases with specific technologies and actors, such as corporations and states, is called for. It is an illusion, however, to believe that ‘we’ free subjects could somehow bring the cyberworld under ‘our’ democratic control. Deeper questioning is necessary, without demanding quick remedies. On the fundamental level, removed from the urgency of pressing, factual, social and political issues, the free movement of resistance consists in the human mind’s movement in thinking in order to understand the nature of movement itself and make the crucial distinction between *productive movement* and the *movement of interplay* as modes of being. Such a distinction is an ontological one that can be seen in simple phenomena themselves, long prior to any algorithmic outsourcing of the control of movements to efficient, autonomous AI, which is a kind of consummation of mathematized, logical control of movement through automation. The ontology of interplay necessitates also a recasting of human being itself from subjectivity, according to which it is human beings themselves as subjects that ultimately underlie the movements of the world. Rather, the human being has to be conceived ontologically as player in the interplay of the world. Ontological insight is a priori, that is, it is prior to any empirical experience of the world in its facticity and, moreover, it already mentally shapes and eidetically defines all such empirical experience, which is necessarily always a posteriori, i.e. after the historical ontological casting. Put more succinctly: ontological thinking casts the historically thinkable. AI algorithms, too, digitize only the empirically given facticity of the world 'after the fact'. Such algorithmized automation easily seduces through the convenience and benefits it can provide, but it also has the darker, insidious side of exposing us to automated movements that we can neither understand nor influence.

The very concept of efficiency and effectiveness itself arises within the ontology of productive movement. It is known under the name of causa efficiens, the Latin term for just one of the four causes first thought through by Aristotle in his ontology of productive movement. The absolute belief in causa efficiens is essential for all modern science, for it is at the heart of its modus operandi, its way of working. Efficient causality goes hand in hand with the age-old, conventional conception of one-dimensional, linear time along with happenings that are ordered sequentially according to this supposed efficient causality. Linear time is simply a way of counting movement along the time-line to assign events to a definite time-number. Reciprocal causality does not break out of linear causality, but only complements it with a law of reaction. Humean scepticism about efficient causality is justified insofar as it cannot be proven, but only firmly believed within a given onto-hermeneutic cast of the world. Hence the philosophical confidence of both British empiricism and American pragmatism. Efficient causality apparently works to all intents and purposes in the case of the natural sciences, but with the advent of sub-atomic physics and its quantum indeterminacy, the question concerning the nature, i.e. the beingness, of movement and time even in the case of physical beings is back on the philosophical agenda. This is the case even though mainstream philosophy of science is oblivious to the question of time and would not touch it even if it were aware of it. Today's mainstream (academic) philosophy has been relegated to the status of handmaiden, or rather whore, to modern science, analogous to the status of medieval philosophy as ancilla theologiae, and it largely accepts its diminished status, contenting itself instead with a more modest, ethical role. When it is not playing the role of auxiliary to science, today's philosophy is engaged in the innocuous scholarly pursuit of talking *about* philosopher-names from the tradition rather than attempting to *think through* the phenomena themselves.

The movement called interplay, by contrast, the sociating, intertwining movement resulting from the interchange among multiple sources of free movement, cannot be assigned simply to an efficient cause. Why? Because the outcome of an intertwining of free movements from independent sources has to be *negotiated* in an *interplay of mutual estimation* among the multiple, free sources of movement themselves which ultimately are we ourselves. Such mutual estimation, entirely absent from the ontology of productive movement, is the key phenomenon in the pivot from an ontology of whatness to one of whoness, on which more shortly. This pivot goes hand in hand with opening up philosophical questioning to the rich phenomenality of interplay-movement, in contradistinction to the traditional epistemological focus on productive movement. If social movement is ever to be adequately conceived, it requires at base an adequate ontology of movement as interplay.

3. Modern Science's Will to Power, Whatness and Whoness

3.1. Can you envisage a future where the definition of humankind itself ever becomes outmoded? Is it possible that we might evolve ourselves into extinction?

The essential defining of humankind itself is always an historical question resting on how the phenomenon of human being itself is interpreted in a given time, a given age or era. Since it is a question of human being itself, it is an ontological question concerning the mode of being of human beings, i.e. their beingness or way of presencing in three-dimensional historical time. The Greek definition of the human being as the animal that has the λόγος (logos), that was translated into Latin as animal rationale, survives today in our thinking ourselves to be rational animals — in my view, an historically outmoded definition. This definition of humankind differs essentially from its (likewise outmoded) Cartesian definition as res cogitans, i.e. the thinking thing, albeit that both are 'what' answers to the question. If the thinking of the thinking thing is conceived as, that is, interpreted as, the computing thing or res computans, then we are already on the way to conceiving ourselves as, in principle, no different from a computer of some kind and issuing a generous, but rash, invitation to AI to make incursions. It is noteworthy that when Turing conceived his Universal Turing Machine to compute computable numbers, the computers he had in mind were first of all the human beings, mostly women, who at that time carried out manual calculations and were called computers. Hence human thinking for him was a matter of computation that could also be done by an artificial computer. The well-known Turing Test is glibly accepted by skipping over the sleight of hand that consists in equating cognition with computation, hence putting machine-being and human being ontologically on the same, thingly footing. This is an ontological question, not an empirical one that could ever be settled by any kind of experiment that proved that a computer was as intelligent as a human being.

Such a conception of human thinking as a kind of computation is by no means obsolete today in a neuroscience that conceives the brain as the, albeit incredibly complex, computing unit of the human being — that Cartesian thinking thing — all within the ambit of efficient, material causality. The very emergence of modern neuroscience is tacitly predicated upon conceiving the human being ontologically as a cogitating thing, thus providing a bridge for technoscience, which is concerned with controlling the movement of things, to invade the mind, now equated with the brain and central nervous system. Like subjective consciousness, such a material computing unit is encapsulated inside, namely, inside the human body. Hence it becomes an obvious move that a digitized computing unit be implanted in the human body, itself on the way to closing the gap between human and machine in cyborgs and opening the way, in particular, to Überveillance. After all, we are purportedly ontologically the same or, even worse, it is blindly assumed that human being is on a par with some kind of computerized being. The firm belief of modern neuroscience — and it is merely an article of faith — is that subjective consciousness and the workings of the brain are somehow equivalent, or at least homœomorphic, with the former being explicable in terms of the latter by way of efficient causality. This does not amount to the extinction of humankind as a species, that is, as a kind of animal, but it certainly amounts to extinguishing human freedom itself as a prelude to putting the painless and unknowingly voluntary extinction of human freedom cybernetically into practice. The present-day concern with the endangerment of survival of the human species itself on the planet due to environmental destruction, especially climate change, is blind to the issue that the extinction of humankind as a species could be averted, but the self-abolition of human being itself be consummated through our own thinking on the basis of a flawed ontology. Conceiving the human being onto-hermeneutically *as* a species of animal is itself a legacy from ancient Greek thinking. An animal is a being animated by an anima, which is the Latin translation of Greek ψυχή (psychae). This anima is then marked by a specific difference, namely nous (Greek) or rationality (Latin), to render it as a *human* animal-being. But is this cast of human being itself adequate to the phenomena themselves? Are we humans at base animals endowed with a rational superstructure?

The age-old debate in anglophone philosophy over freedom vs. determinism is strongly defined and encouraged by the rise of Newtonian mathematized physics and the extension of this wonderous, apparently new discovery by Newton, to all kinds of scientific endeavour including, in particular, in psychology. The laws of motion governing physical motion became the blueprint for a science of psychology that was to causally explain human behaviour, and this dream of causal explanation, and hence control over human life-movements, is by no means defunct today. On the contrary, it is driving the development of AI. The same emulation of physic's laws of motion has been and continues to be practised in other social sciences such as economics, especially in its mathematized variants. Digital algorithms are called on today to predict human behaviour, invariably in the name of enhancing 'our' convenience, well-being and security. An example of such a scientific psychological endeavour is predictive or pre-emptive policing that implicitly assumes ontologically that the human being is not the free source of its own movements and hence, in principle, humans' life-movements can be precalculated once 'we' get the algorithms up to speed to make predictions of individual behaviour on the basis of mined mountains of digital data collected about the behaviour of a given individual from a given population. This is a task assigned to behavioural biometrics. But who are we? A thing whose movements are governed ultimately by some intricate laws of behaviour? And what does human freedom mean? These questions are relegated to the realm of 'philosophical speculation' that modern science dismisses as superfluous and fanciful or, at best, as a pastime. The absolute will to power over movement makes short shrift of such roadblocks to scientific progress.

3.2. You argue that science claims "the absolute will to effective power over all kinds of movement and change". What is wrong with this claim? Does it necessarily preclude any other forms of 'knowing'?

I do indeed say that modern science is driven by the absolute will to effective power over all kinds of movement and change, which is a hidden metaphysical will taking the place of the θεός (theos) or god in the older metaphysics. It is not so much a matter of arguing logically, especially in any adversarial sort of way, as it is an attempt to bring certain elementary, but decisive phenomena to light so they can be clearly seen. Metaphysics itself, as can be studied in Aristotle's *Metaphysics*, consists of two parts: ontology and theology, i.e. the investigation of beings simply insofar as they are beings, and the investigation of the nature of a supreme instance, the 'divine', that may well not be a being. Beings qua beings have several different modes of being, which Aristotle investigates systematically. Very briefly: the first mode of being involves the elementary categories through which a being can be addressed and understood, such as what it is (its essence), how it is (quality), how much it is (quantity), where it is (place), how it is in relation to another being, etc. The second mode of being is whether the being comes to presence of itself or only incidentally. The third is whether the being presents itself as it truly is or falsely, distortedly as it is *not*. And finally, beings presence in movement according to potentiality, energetic activity and finished presence. As I have already laid out, the paradigm which Aristotle had in mind for such an ontology of movement is that of productive movement as exemplified in the technique or art of carpentry or house-building. Such a movement is productive, under the control of an efficient cause, namely the carpenter's or builder's know-how, and results in the completed presence of a finished product such as a table, an efficiently transformed form of the initial material, wood. The movement of the making itself with the carpenter working on the wood (the material cause or causa materialis) that is to become a table is the energy or, literally, the at-work-ness of the potentiality itself, which is the know-how.

There is nothing 'wrong' in itself with this ontology of productive movement,which is the germ of all the technological achievements of Western humankind throughout the centuries. The productive, foreknowing control of movement at the core of Western epistemology is doubtless beneficial in myriad ways and has spread globally. We all have an interest in things being produced, and produced well and efficiently, in order to live well. However, this conception of movement as productive and controllable from a source becomes problematic when it is totalized to all phenomena of movement under the impetus of the will to effective power over movement. The reason for this is that such an ontology of productive movement and change does violence to all those movements that do not fit the productive paradigm. Such is the case with our sharing the world with one another in all kinds of interplay which calls on us to learn to see and appreciate more clearly the mutual esteem and estimation at play in such interplay. Only then can social movement be adequately conceived without attempting to force the square ontological peg of productive movement into the round hole of mutually estimative, social interplay which is the movement where trust has its place among us. I emphasize the mutuality of interplay, i.e. what we can do for each other, rather than setting up the usual moralistic opposition between altruism and egoism. In daily life it is mutuallty that facllltates our sharlng the world.

3.3. If we are to push back these claims of absoluteness or arrogations to power by technoscience, you speak of making "room for something else". What do you mean?

To put it very succinctly, most movements and changes in the world with which we are entirely familiar on a factual (ontic) everyday level are not of the kind that is amenable to the ontology of productive, effective, efficient movement. All sociating movement, for instance, already breaks the mould of productive movement. In particular, all politics are movements of (inevitably rivalrous) interplay rather than productive, effective, efficient movements emanating from a single source, not even if that source is an authoritarian dictator with an iron grip on his repressive state apparatuses. This is very well-known as a matter of fact (ontically), say, among all political commentators and political scientists (politics is a power game), but it is entirely unknown ontologically. Philosophy always has the task of bringing what is well-known implicitly and ontically to its explicit ontological interpretation. Hence it may seem to be doing something superfluous and to be dealing with trivialities and banalities. The phenomenon of interplay, however, demands an alternative ontology which is "something else", hitherto unknown in traditional metaphysical ontology. All modern science, although it is today entirely oblivious to its millennia-old metaphysical legacy, implicitly assumes an ontology of productive, effective movement with the final aim of predicting it, controlling it. Without such an aim of effective control, it would not count as science but be rejected as empirically untested or unverifiable speculation, or a waste of time. It is also noteworthy that everyday discourse is habitually concerned with opining and fretting about what will happen on all levels, even if it is a question about what the weather will be like next week, whose answer is provided these days by the science of meteorology. Why this fixation on what will happen tomorrow rather than learning to see elementary phenomena themselves in their simplicity?

3.4. What do you mean when you say that there is a difference between "thinking about society" and "thinking society"? Why is this distinction important in our times?

"Thinking about society" is what sociology and historiography do in the vein of explaining happenings, i.e. movements, in society and putting some sort of coherent narrative on factual happenings. Such endeavours remain within the empiricist tradition akin to common sense, which has dominated the anglophone philosophical tradition since Francis Bacon's works in the early seventeenth century, at the latest. "Thinking society" is an entirely different, philosophical endeavour that attempts to adequately conceptualize the modes of being of social phenomena, especially that of *sociation* itself, which is the movement through which we human beings share the world with one another. We are entirely familiar with modes of sociation and understand them very well, but we do not know what they are *as* modes of being or even what modes of being is supposed to mean in this context. The enterprise is socio-ontological and depends therefore on the fundamental ontological difference between beings and their mode of being, i.e. between beings and as what (or as who) they are interpreted to be in an elementary way in a given historical age. Hence, for example, the mode of being of human beings in our present age is interpreted to be subjects endowed with an internal consciousness vis-à-vis an external, objective world. This onto-hermeneutic cast of human being remains open to questioning as long as there is genuine philosophical thinking.

The distinction is important because, in the absence of an adequate ontology of the sociating movement of interplay, all movement and change in the world is interpreted by default in terms of cause and effect along linear time rather than as an incalculable interplay within the openness of three-dimensional time. Social interplay itself is played out among whos, not whats, which represents a monumental shift for conceiving society and social movement. All interplay among whos is mutually estimative, on which more shortly.

3.5. Why do you say that the modern mind-set, whether it be scientific or philosophical mainstream, is not interested in posing simple ontological questions regarding *who* we are, rather than *what* we are?

The modern mind-set is well-content with the onto-hermeneutic cast of the human being as conscious subject, i.e. as a kind of what, for it is entirely compatible with and amenable to control in line with the venerable ontology of productive movement. This is the status quo that goes along with the complacency and smugness of a scientific attitude that 'we' will make endless further progress in controlling movement, today with the help of AI. All the scientific institutes, including universities, have a vested interest in maintaining the status quo on which they thrive. The misgivings about these totalizing ambitions of modern science are shunted off to an extra area of moral and ethical concern to somehow rein in the hubris intoxicating modern science, including neuroscience in particular. Asserting moral values and ethical concerns about what 'ought' to be, however, is rather like shutting the stable door after the horse has bolted, rendering ethics as a kind of injunctive or prohibitive afterthought. In my view, the question of values is an eminently socio-ontological task to be tackled starting from the key phenomenon of mutually estimative interplay of powers in which both things and people, whats and whos, are evaluated and valued.

3.6. Furthermore, what exactly do you mean when you speak of a 'social ontology of whoness'?

I have already said something briefly about the task of a social ontology consisting in thinking through modes of sociation, which are movements of interplay. But why whoness? First of all because, already in our naïve, everyday understanding, there is a more or less obvious distinction made as a matter of course, in both our thinking and our behaviour, between what and who. Whats are things and whos are persons (a somewho 'ought' to be accorded the value of human dignity, which implicitly presupposes whoness). The ontological questions are then: What is the mode of being of whats, i.e. what is whatness? And what is the mode of being of whos, i.e. what is whoness? At this point it becomes apparent that, whereas the question of whatness has received lavish attention in the metaphysical tradition for over two millennia, the question of whoness is still fighting for a place on the philosophical agenda. The word 'whatness' translates into Latin 'quidditas' which, in turn, renders Greek τό τι ἦν εἶναι (to ti aen einai) or οὐσία (ousia), i.e. the *essence* of a thing. In asking the philosophical question, What is X?, the answer runs along the lines of saying what its essence is. There is nothing in the philosophical tradition that parallels this questioning in the realm of the alternative question, Who is Y? The answer given is inevitably a certain individual person's name, such as Socrates. This simple answer evades the question concerning the whoness of Socrates or any other human being as a mode of being. In fact, the very project of ontology initiated by Aristotle forecloses the posing of the question of whoness (Latin: quissitas) as a mode of being in its own right from the very start with its fundamental concept, viz. οὐσία (ousia), which is traditionally translated as 'substance'. Whoness, however, is a phenomenon that must be approached *relatively*, namely, as mutually estimative interplay. Put another way: a who has no substance.

Aristotle goes into great detail in the *Metaphysics* investigating the nature of οὐσία (ousia) as the primary and leading ontological category, an investigation with considerable repercussions for all of Western thinking thereafter. The οὐσία of a being is defined by its λόγος (logos) specifying its essence as an εἶδος (eidos), literally, as a 'look' of whatness that a being presents to the mind. Aristotle proceeds from specifying the whatness of non-living things to living things whose οὐσία, namely, the ψυχή (psychae), renders them as living with the power, or δύναμις (dynamis), of self-movement in nourishing themselves, growing and decaying, and also reproducing themselves. Animals are those living beings with the additional power of moving their own location. Finally, the beingness of the human being is defined to be that of a kind or species of animal, but with the additional differentiating faculty of νοῦς (nous), i.e. of an understanding mind (λόγος in the sense of reason). There is thus a stepwise hierarchy of determination of essence from inanimate things, to animate things (plants and animals) and finally, to the animate thing endowed with a thinking mind, which specifies human being with its specific difference within the genus of animals. The οὐσία or beingness of the human being is therefore, for Aristotle, a kind of whatness, without the question of the whoness of human beings ever being raised. It is entirely questionable whether Aristotle's stepwise, bottom-up procedure to conceptualize the beingness of the human being as a species of animal is adequate to the phenomenon of human being itself. That is, it is questionable whether the bottom-up ontological procedure is ever able to reach the whoness of human being itself since it seems unable to escape the orbit of whatness.

An alternative is a top-down progression from human being itself conceived hermeneutically first of all as having an openness to three-dimensional time, i.e. an existential exposure to 3D-time. It should be noted that 'existence' from the Latin signifies literally a 'standing-out', an 'ex-sisting'. This is why Heidegger's conception of human being itself, which he calls Dasein in *Being and Time*, is characterized as existence, i.e. as a standing-out or exposure to three-dimensional, "originary time" (*Being and Time*) which is nothing other than the Da of Dasein itself. Within this three-dimensional temporal Da, human beings encounter both things and others, whats and whos, which are all interrelated within the world. This world itself assumes shape and is understood hermeneutically AS such-and-such within a given historical age, i.e. within three-dimensional time. The capitalized AS here is the hermeneutic AS on which all understanding by the mind depends. From this perspective it can be seen that from the start the mind is conceived as shared and not as somehow enclosed within an individual consciousness. Within this alternative approach to conceiving human being itself first of all as existential exposure to three-dimensional time, it becomes questionable whether it is at all sensible to speak of humankind as a 'species' with its own specific difference (rationality) within a genus (animal) as Aristotle and Western thinking do right up to today's science. Even ethics adopts the conception of human beings as a species. There is today, for instance, an ethical concern with the 'survival of the human species' in the face of environmental degradation and catastrophic climate change. This leaves open the question whether the survival of the human species could go along with unwittingly willed extinction of human being itself.

If, alternatively, human being itself is cast hermeneutically as existential exposure to three-dimensional time, then this temporal openness becomes the playground in which the social interplay among human beings is played out. Such interplay as the characteristic sociating movement of societies necessarily involves mutually estimating, evaluating, esteeming *who* we are, not *what* we are. Hence a genuine phenomenology of whoness becomes possible and, indeed, imperative.

3.7. How do you approach the question of identity from a social ontology of whoness?

The question of identity is that of the constitution of selfhood. With subjective self-consciousness one has only the reflective bending-back of consciousness onto itself as a kind of observer, as a conscience within the individual subject. Hence Kant's morality is concerned with the internal conscience of a subject critically observing and judging its own actions. Once the insight into existential whoness arises, the self of somewho (in contrast to somewhat, something) is no longer solely this reflective bending-back onto itself, but a reflection from the world, above all, from the world of others who estimate either appreciatively or depreciatively who you are, thus affirming or negating your stand as a self in the shared world. Things (somewhats), by contrast, are unable to see themselves in a reflection from the world. Your self comes to stand through an appropriation of existential possibilities reflected from the world and in power interplay with it. Hence self-identity always involves difference; identity is always such via the other. Who you imagine yourself to be in your own self-reflective estimation may stand in crass contradiction with who the world of others estimates and esteems you to be, for instance, in today's digital social media (cyber-bullying). The difference inherent in identity may thus become a painful contradiction, such as depression, pushing for resolution. Since your identity as self is a belonging-together of your self-casting with possibilities on offer from the world in your time, it may be multiple, resulting in a broken identity that allows differing perspectives on the world. Hence, for example, a migrant living in another country and culture has the 'gift' of a broken, rather than a monolithic identity, whereas a nationalist's self-adopted identity may have more coherence at the price of narrow-minded experience of the world's diverse possibilities.

The world itself is embedded in the three-dimensional time of history with its moods and modes of understanding within which potentials for existing as self emerge and offer themselves. You exist, leading your life and casting yourself into existential possibilities opening up from the temporal dimension of the future. In your free self-movement, you are a source of power, i.e. of potency or δύναμις, residing first of all in your abilities. Your self emerges from what you can appropriate for your self as your very own singular possibilities for existing in the world of your time in a power interplay with others in which they may either encourage or discourage you, further or thwart you. In this broad sense, your coming to your self-stand in the world is a power struggle. You may wager the casting of a singular self, or you may cast yourself into those average, 'normal' options for existing opened up by the world that offer less resistance. In either case, your freedom does not consist in your being able to move and cast yourself arbitrarily without meeting any resistance from the world of others, but in what you manage to negotiate in the existential interplay.

4. Questions of Ethics and Power

4.1. Is there still room in our time for serious philosophical and theological investigations? That is, are the 'big' questions still relevant?

The 'big' questions are still relevant, but for whom? They are highly relevant to those whom they concern, who may be very few, singular selves in our time. But our time is not eternity, and historical time throws up very different configurations. I can't say much at all about theology except to note that what I call the absolute will to effective power over all kinds of movement and change is the unseen god, the technogod of the modern scientific age, whom I have dubbed Willy P., in which all of us have an interest. Aristotle's alternative god conceived as the 'look of the fair' (εἶδος τοῦ καλοῦ, eidos tou kalou), serving as telos for the movement of the world, has an entirely different flavour. The word καλός (kalos, fair) in ancient Greek signifies a quality of both aesthetic and ethical beauty, just as 'fair' does in English. In Aristotelean terms, the 'look', 'sight' (εἶδος) or idea of the fair is both the eidetic (causa formalis) and teleological cause (causa finalis) of the world's movement, and by no means an efficient cause, a maker. This sight can only be seen as an idea by the mind, i.e. by nous that on the whole is continually, energetically at work, whereas we individuals participate only intermittently in this shared nous and have in mind the sight, i.e. the idea of the fair to hold in high esteem and guide our actions. The sight of the fair is complemented by its negation, the sight of the foul, that often intermingles confusingly with the sight of the fair.

The technogod I have called Willy P. is the sight, or idea, of unbridled, effective mastery of movement on which our modern mind is absolutely fixated, Willy P. has a close brother whom I call Pleon Exia, who is the god we have in mind when striving to have ever more. Pleon Exia comes from the ancient Greek πλεονεξία signifying 'grasping greediness, gain, advantage, striving to have a larger share'. Pleon Exia is the god motivating the gainful game (see more on this below), on whose sight all players in the game are fixated. How the game is played among the players can be either fair or foul. Its foulness being fired by self-interest that often tips over into ruthlessness, whereas fairness is now the modified idea of the fair under which the players estimate and esteem each other appropriately, appreciatively, with the Goddess of Fairness (akin to Ἀστρθαία) looking on approvingly from the heavens.

On the side of ontology, there is room for thinking on how the beingness of beings, (their onto-hermeneutic 'looks') is to be recast in our own age, even if this room is occupied only by a rare few who are seismically sensitive to the messages of the Zeit-Geist and co-casting our historical future. It may or may not be that a later age finds this ontological recasting highly pertinent and distressingly necessary, especially if and when the absolute belief in efficient control over movement and the striving for more and more give way to misgivings. In the first place, there is the hubris inherent in the absolute will to power over all kinds of movement, even to the extent of manipulating the reproduction of living organisms, thus interfering with the intricate interconnections and equilibria of nature. This will to power is supplemented by the insatiable appetite to appropriate thingified value that drives the gainful game, as I will touch on below. The step back from the hubristic will to power over movement alters the very character of thinking itself from that of intellectual prowess in mastering problems of control to a thoughtful thanking, or thankfully thinking, the givenness of human being itself as 3D-temporal openness for the world. Human being as this openness is the given gift to which, by thinking, we respond with thanks. Who we are as human beings depends upon the thoughtful thanks and thankful thought we return for this gift.

In the second place, a step back from the absolute will to power over movement reveals whoness in contradistinction to whatness. Whoness can only be conceived by thinking through the phenomena of estimative interplay among us human beings sharing the world in a given age. This interplay is a movement sui generis of mutual estimation of who each of us is, ranging over the entire gamut from highly appreciative esteem to savagely depreciative misesteem with many subtle variants (such as backhanded compliments) in between. Because mutual estimation is an essential feature of interplay among human beings, it cannot be controlled and manipulated like the interaction among things, and attempts to do so amount to a perversion of its character. What is esteemed or misesteemed, appreciated or depreciated in such interplay, from which values arise, are, first of all, each individual's respective powers and abilities. As with productive movement, all interplay comes about through the exercise of powers, potentials which in this case are multiple and intertwining, partly co-operative, partly opposed. As such, with this broad conception of powers, all interplay is an unpredictable power play of multiple powers, and individual powers and abilities (comprising more than just productive powers, i.e. productive skills) are sociated via this *mutually estimative power interplay*.

Social powers, however, are not exhausted by individuals' powers and abilities, for there are other social powers whose social ontology must be thought through in their own right, notably, the power of thingified value in its various forms or 'looks', starting with money and money income, and through to the political power exercised by the government and the state. Money as the crystalline form of thingified value, for instance, can be conceived initially as the medium mediating the interchange of human powers and abilities and the product thereof. As thingifed value it serves to obscure and cover up what lies beneath, namely, the mutual estimation of powers and abilities. Such thingified value covers up the estimation of whoness with an estimation of whatness. In this sense, thingified value could even be termed whatified value.

Money's power as "universal equivalent" (Marx), however, reaches far beyond this mediation into all sorts of corruption and criminality. Perverse intertwinings of personal powers and abilities can arise between the power of money and the power wielded by political office. *Plutocracy*, for instance, is an intertwining of the power of wealth with political power, perhaps by an individual whose inherent personal abilities are meagre but is able to buy status-certification, such as university degrees, through devious means. Or power in world politics can be exercised via the medium of thingified value, e.g. through sanctions being imposed on transactions through the US-dollar-dominated international banking system, which amounts to a modern form of imperialism without the need the establish colonies. All organizations, of course, whether they be intranational or international, engage in their own power interplays with other organizations and politics, as well as in their own internal power struggles.

An appreciation of the movement of mutually estimative power interplay, which, as I have attempted to show, has an entirely different ontology from that of efficient, productive movement, can also open insights into how things in the world as a whole, including especially the Earth and all living beings, are estimated and appreciated in interplay among us humans. Such an appreciation of the Earth as a whole with its plants and animals is a consequence of interrogating philosophically in what whoness, in contradistinction to whatness, consists. Instead of regarding the Earth as a multitude of resources to be productively exploited and of living organisms to be productively manipulated in the gainful game of capitalism, it can be valued in the sense of being appreciated and esteemed for itself and its offering the places where we live, and can live well, with one another. Thingified value serves to obscure the Earth's value to us in dwelling on it by engendering an unbridled lust for gain through exploiting the Earth's resources. In this context, the Earth could even be appreciated and esteemed via the medium of thingified value, provided the veil of thingified value is drawn aside. Putting a price on carbon dioxide emissions, for example, can be a way of esteeming and appreciating the Earth by sparing it the convulsions of climate change that ravage plant and animal life on Earth. Sparing the Earth for its own sake should be distinguished from a struggle to secure the survival of the human species. The precondition for such appropriate estimation of the Earth presupposes that the obfuscation generated by the fetishism of thingified value is seen through.

4.2. Are ethics as a body of moral principles 'expiring'? If not, where do we turn for ethical values, or at least an ethical system which will underlay technical standards?

Ethics as a body of moral principles could well be 'expiring'. The most famous and original ethics are those of Aristotle in which his ontology of productive movement is also silently at work, if only because he has no ontology of the movement of interplay, even when he comes to considering phenomena that are expressly interplay, say, in his consideration of commutative justice or the art of rhetoric. The Greek word for such commutation is συναλλαγή (synallagae) which means 'interchange,' i.e. sociating interplay. The interchange of views and interchange of goods (commerce, trade) are conspicuous features of social living not only in the West. In fact, such interchange could be said to sociate societies. Commericial transactions can be regarded, on the one hand, as the way a merchant makes money and, on the other, also as the way productive powers of all kinds are exercised for mutual benefit through money-mediated interchange.

The neglect of an ontology of sociating interplay renders ethics themselves as a separate department of philosophical endeavour that has been preserved ever since the Greek beginnings, thus relegating ethics themselves to the derivative status of an afterthought. In a certain way I see ethics being superseded by a social ontology of whoness whose kernel is an ontology of mutually estimative power interplay, a kind of movement in its own right. How mutually estimative power interplays play out are ethical questions of 'values'. Or rather conversely, ethical questions of 'values' are questions concerning how mutually estimative power interplays are played out, fairly or not. Our values as they are lived in customs comprising the shared habitual practices of a culture shift historically according to the outcomes of social struggles over values. For instance, that women have come to be valued ethically as political citizens with a vote is the outcome of centuries of social and political struggle. And questions of 'values' must not exclude thingified value as one form or 'look' of value, as if money ('filthy lucre') were beyond the ethical pale. Such an ontology of interplay represents an as yet ignored, but nonetheless serious philosophical challenge to the silently reigning dominance of the ontology of productive power. The first step remains: learning to see this clearly. Our human freedom relies fundamentally on our seeing clearly so as to orient our life-movements, including our life-movements of resistance. Otherwise we exist in cloudy unclarity and a panoply of self-delusions that serve to confuse and thus prop up the status quo.

4.3. Are 'data ethics' increasingly replacing 'people ethics'?

'Data ethics' are an illusion emanating from the replication of the world in an artificial, surrogate, digitized cyberworld inhabited by digital data and digital algorithms, both of which are basically binary numbers, or bit-strings, thus fulfilling the Pythagorean dream that the essence of the world is number. Who we are as people thus gains a digitized representation within the cyberworld that can be further calculated and algorithmically manipulated and finally played back into our shared physical world with enormous effect, for the algorithms are increasingly in the position to control our existential life-movements, enabling or restricting them. In particular, your *reputation* as somewho and your very identity have their representation in the cyberworld. This cyberworld reputation increasingly supersedes your 'real world' reputation in gossip, hearsay and the like, even to the point that your cyberworld reputation (say, on social media) can undermine your very self-esteem and destroy you. 'Data ethics' are really 'people ethics' in another, digitized guise. And 'people ethics' are in truth a matter of considering the ongoing mutually estimative power interplays among people that are today being played out more and more via their digitized proxies.

4.4. Are we building an 'electrified ghetto' where the best opportunities are increasingly only available to an elite group? That is, are we unwittingly (or perhaps wittingly) creating more and more disempowered groups?

The first question is who 'we' are, and whether this 'we' is in truth a 'they'. I am often consternated by the continual talk in the media about what 'we' are doing or not doing for the bad or good of society or the world, or about opinions 'we' hold, where I say to myself, I am not part of this falsely presumed 'we'. The media talk constantly in pandering terms of this fake 'we' that we are supposed to be in liberal democratic societies, even though the gulf between a political power elite and the rest of the populace remains. Be that as it may, those who are savvy about the existential possibilities opened up by the cyberworld may well be at an advantage in the estimative power plays to earn a living, gain status as somewho, win fame and celebrity status, or lasso some political power since power interplays are increasingly being played out via digitized proxies. The multitude of power plays in the world inevitably generates uneven outcomes, with some doing better than others, either fairly or by skulduggery. One major issue is whether there is a permeability for entering promising power plays in the cyberworld, or whether there are unfair barriers in place enabling some kind of elite to establish itself behind them. The erection of such barriers depends decisively on the power of thingified value. Racial prejudice, for instance, operates mostly in insidious, tacit ways that amount to depreciating and excluding the other simply as a matter of course. I don't think there are disempowered groups, but only downtrodden and demoralized groups who do not realize their particular powers and exercise them. As long as we are alive, we have power of movement in all sorts of ways. Social and political power struggles may be, and mostly are, long, arduous and bitter, with repeated setbacks. Already today they are conducted within the medium of the cyberworld, and thus are subject to all its possibilities of algorithmic manipulation.

4.5. What consequences does a socio-ontology of whoness have for thinking through what a capitalist economy is?

I rename capitalism the *gainful game* in the following sense: The augmentation of thingified value in its circular movement that is the circuit of capital itself, is enabled by the mutually estimative, competitive power interplays mediating this movement involving multiple value-form transformations. These include first of all the interplay between buyers and sellers of goods and services on various markets through which their exchange-values are mutually estimated and come about, including quantitatively in price. Goods and services offered on the market are at first only *potential* exchange-values; they gain a *finished presence* or entelechy in *actually* being sold for a price. An enterprise has to purchase its means of production and raw materials on the appropriate markets and organize its supply chains. There is no substance (οὐσία) of exchange-value but only its emergence relationally through the interplay itself.

A second interplay is that between the enterprises hiring labour power and its lenders, who are employees of all kinds, from lowly workers up to top managers. This interplay determines the value of labour powers (wages and salaries) and thus also the *income* of employees. Such interplay frequently becomes a tough power struggle in which, in particular, the employers strive to diminish employees' power by preventing unions from being established. The borrowers and lenders of money-capital also enter a power interplay with one another (mostly via the market) over interest income, just as the lessees and lessors of land do over land rents. The gainful game is at core the competitive power interplay over *earning income* of the four basic kinds: wages, interest, ground-rent and the residual profit of enterprise (partly distributed as dividends), all of which are forms, or 'looks' of thingified value. In addition, there are numerous hybrids of these four basic forms. Thingified value comes about through the competitive estimative interplay over incomes as the medium for this interplay. The capitalist enterprise is the lead player in the gainful game, for it brings the other income-earning players together and pushes to generate the revenues from which all the other incomes (wages, ground rent and interest) have to be paid, leaving the residue of profit of enterprise. The enterprise is therefore generally the most aggressive player. The players in the gainful game are motivated to a greater or lesser extent by the lust for gain, the striving for more and more. Money as the crystalline thingification of value serves as a motivating, fetishized, greatly desired thing whose fetishization can go so far that the desirous player lusting for gain even derives his or her selfhood by identifying with the acquisition and accumulation of this valued thing. Once again, whoness is perverted by whatness.

One of the fundamental widespread misconceptions today is that of economic growth, which is invariably conceived as some kind of material increase, especially in the sheer amount of goods produced and natural resources consumed. But economic growth is the augmentative generation of thingified value in interplay, a social quantity, not a physical one. Conceptually speaking, the elementary, core interplay (via the medium of thingified value) is that between players exercising their powers and abilities for their mutual benefit. Thus it consists in a mutual estimation of their whoness insofar as your stand as somewho depends on how your individual powers and abilities are esteemed and valued, including monetarily. In this elementary sense, there is no limit to what we can do for each other through mutual esteem. A major impediment to economic well-being is the depreciatory estimation of individuals' abilities, more often than not for the sake of economic gain (especially entrepreneurs' depressing workers' wages to a paltry minimum). Such a conception of economic growth differs essentially from a conception whereby it consists in ever more rapacious exploitation of the Earth's resources. This is capitalism as seen through the ontology of productive power.[4] The gainful game, however, is the same kind of (capitalist) economy seen through the ontology of power interplay. The misconception of thingified value (say, as a *substance* extracted from workers' labour) thus has major deleterious consequences in today's debates over the so-called ecological limits to growth by distorting the view of key phenomena: the augmentation of thingified value must not be equated to intensified exploitation of the Earth. The augmentation of thingified value is a deceptive cover for how we humans can increasingly benefit each other through the mutual exercise of our individual powers and abilities of all kinds, and such augmentation does not necessarily require increased exploitation of the Earth (its resources), but can proceed whilst learning to spare it and cherish it as the place where we dwell. Power struggles to spare the Earth from savage exploitation for the sake of gain run in parallel with key income-earning struggles in the gainful game over fair outcomes (especially with regard to wages and working conditions).

4.6. What are some of the problems of an economy being primarily based on digital technology?

I take digital technology to be today synonymous with the cyberworld, first of all as a state of mind, namely, our own historical mind-set. The global economy is a capitalist one based on the circular,

---

4 The major shortcoming of Heidegger's engagement with Marx is that Heidegger views Marx's critique of capitalism solely through the lens of the ontology of productive movement. Hence capitalism is conceiverd as part of the Gestell, the set-up, whereas in truth, it is essentually the gainful game, as outlined above. Cf. my *Capital and Technology: Marx and Heidegger* Röll Verlag, Dettelbach 2000 (in German), 3rd ed. CreateSpace, North Charleston 2015 (English and German).

self-augmenting movement of thingified value in its various guises, i.e. value-forms, of money, goods, production processes, wages, profit of enterprise, ground-rent, finance capital, interest, and so on. This constitutes the gainful game in the medium of thingified value. Because such thingified, thingified value in its various forms or 'looks' is essentially quantifiable and thus easily digitizable, it is amenable to becoming a 'citizen' of the cyberworld, circulating along with other bit-strings. An obvious example is everything to do with banking and finance, which deal in pure thingified value in its monetary form, thus enabling all monetary movements to be efficiently controlled by the appropriate algorithms. Such increases in efficiency in the banking and finance spheres are equivalent to profit-enhancing productivity increases.

On the material side of the value-augmenting, circular movement of capital there are, above all, the logistics of digitally managing the flow of materials and goods within the supply chains for today's global production processes and also deliveries to stores and customers. The efficiency of logistics operations is greatly enhanced by the cyberworld with its possibilities of automated cybernetic control. The circulation processes of capital such as carrying out transactions and accounting can also be optimized by employing the appropriate algorithms in the guise of, say, online shops and sophisticated accounting software.

The movement of thingified value digitized into bit-strings can be made vastly more efficient by employing productive algorithms to control processes, but no amount of clever algorithms can ever master the interplay of the value-transformation, especially of goods and services into money, i.e. their sale, in which buyer and seller must negotiate an agreement under the conditions of competitive market interplay. Another exemplary sticking-point is the loan of capital that likewise must be mediated by an interplay between lender and borrower over terms and conditions, especially interest rates. Such interplay is essentially incalculable in advance and hence non-digitizable, despite all efforts to do so. Shares in public companies, too, are traded worldwide on stock exchanges today with the aid of algorithms designed to make trading profits. These myriads of algorithms, however, including high frequency trading algorithms, are often caught on the back foot due to unpredictable swings of sentiment in the stock market. Hence digitization of the capitalist economy cannot ever result in its smooth, efficient ticking-over of capital valorization under the sure control of clever algorithms. The market interplay on all sorts of markets is essentially exposed to contingency.

The emergence of the cyberworld as a major playing field for playing the gainful game of capitalism, especially by creating a global mass market, represents an enormous challenge of adaptation on the part of all the players in the gainful game, who comprise just about all of us, since we all require income. The shift causes disruption to many established branches of industry and commerce, especially through the speed at which this shift is taking place. This gives rise to political tensions, including loud calls for protectionism, especially in connection with globalization, because digitized technologies deployed in the cyberworld enable, in particular, globalized sourcing, with consequences for domestic labour-power markets (meagre wages, poor working conditions, unemployment) that lose out in the competitive interplay.

4.7. Can you say more about the connection between the cyberworld and the gainful game?

The cyberworld consists of trillions of strings of binary digits (bits) continually copulating with one another in Turing machines to progenerate further strings of binary digits for the sake of steering movements of all kinds. Even our own identities have become such bit-strings through which we are caught up in the progenerative movement of the copulating bit-strings. On the other side, the gainful game is played in the medium of thingified value which, as quantifiable, has an affinity to the bit-strings continually copulating and thus controlling movements throughout the cyberworld and its physical environs. In this way, the augmentative movement of thingified value we call circuits of capital, has a close affinity to the movement of the cyberworld itself, for the algorithms can assist in enhancing the effectivity of both production and circulation processes of thingified value-in-process. The gainful game thus becomes the *gainful cybergame*, whose turnover-movement dictates the breathless movement of our own lives.

Ever since its inception, the cyberworld with its automated, algorithmic control of movement has been lauded as a great achievement of the human mind, enhancing our lives with conveniences and extending the realm of human freedom. Are these trillions of algorithmically copulating bit-strings steering movements for our sake, or is the cyberworld such only for the sake of the freedom of movement of bit-strings themselves in close co-ordination with the maximally efficient circling of augmenting thingified value? Are we humans in truth only appendages of the digitial devices that integrate us into the cyberworld, merely deluding ourselves that we are or could be, say, democratically in control as the underlying subjects of these movements? Is the gainful game of capitalism, with its continual augmentative movement of thingified value, such for the sake of the enhancement of our human life-movements, or is it rather the other way round: that we humans are players caught in a thingified value-game that is beyond human control? Is it in truth the freedom of movement of thingified value that directs the world's movement and is primary? And is this socio-ontological truth covered up with our own delusions of freedom as human subjects?

To see this clearly (as a necessary precondition for our own freedom), we need to slowly learn to see through the fetishizing veil of thingified value to what lies hidden behind, namely, our own powers and abilities, along with the natural gifts of the Earth, and how we estimate and esteem these powers and gifts. The topsy-turvy world of thingified value bloating itself in passing through its circuits is thus turned the right way up for us to see ourselves in mutually estimative interplay with one another, esteeming, estimating, evaluating each other's powers and potentials as well as their exercise. As long as the interplay is fair it is also where trust is engendered.

4.8. What is the difference between information and knowledge? What are some of the dangers for a society that is increasingly reliant on information to the detriment of knowledge?

Information arises when a form is impressed into a material medium thus leaving behind differences that are interpreted as signs for the λόγος (logos), i.e. for language, expressing some statement of fact or other. Digitized information is composed of binary digits or bits (the basic difference between 0 and 1) impressed into an electronic medium that are interpreted by our human mind as expressing a fact about the state of the world. For instance, I look at my digital watch and interpret the different marks impressed in the electronic medium as a certain time of day. Information in this sense is endless, amounting to an ever-mounting heap of factual statements about the world. If these factual statements are to proceed beyond a jumble of bald facts stored in petabytes of data, they have to be incorporated into some theory or other to bring them into meaningful relation to each other. The theoretical models organizing such information into knowledge about the world are today of the scientific, evidence-based kind. The factual evidence can be biased in many deceptive ways. The modern sciences are at heart all empiricist, working up factual information provided by experience into a theoretical model explaining causally, in some sense, movements in the world. Such scientific theoretical models may be more or less elaborately discursive and their basic concepts may be more or less profound. A scientific, empirically based psychological theory including elements of the neuroscience of early brain development, for instance, may explain how young children growing up in certain social environments may be prone to depression, thus deriving how this proneness can be remedied by a certain therapy. For this, many data must be collected in a proper, experimentally designed manner and analyzed by statistical methods to ascertain regularities. These collected data are the raw information required to input into a theoretical method to test its effectiveness in accounting for the observed phenomenon of depression and also the therapy's effectiveness in remedying this malady. Hence empiricist scientific knowledge goes hand in hand with information because it relies on empirical data, which today are digital data. The evidence base for empiricist science always consists of copious empirical studies collecting data.

The theoretical models employed by such empirically based science, however, inevitably employ certain indispensable, basic concepts that they themselves do not and cannot clarify because they are not given a posteriori (after the event) by experience but are posited a priori to set the theory up in the first place. In the case of psychology, for instance, the fundamental concept is that of psyche itself, but this science proceeds only from a rough and ready, common sense, fuzzy definition of the human psyche without much elaboration, invariably assuming some sort of unclarified interconnection between the brain and the psyche that is inevitably equated with consciousness. It does not and, as empirical science, cannot pose the question, What is the psyche? The question is outside its purview. As I have pointed out earlier, the question is an ontological one relating to the very mode of being of human beings, their beingness. For psychoanalytic theory, for instance, which in a way is more profound than empirical psychology, the psyche is composed firstly of consciousness and the unconscious, but what these latter two are, are similarly ontological questions that only philosophy ever raises. The *question concerning consciousness* remains a big open question also in mainstream philosophy which has enormous problems in fruitfully pursuing it. This is because mainstream philosophy has a very stunted understanding of ontology, lacking as it does any conception of the ontological difference between beings and their beingness inaugurated already by Aristotle. For this mainstream philosophy, ontology has become the trifling enterprise of inquiring into what exists, without ever remotely posing the fundamental question concerning the meaning of being or the meaning of existence. These are enormous philosophical deficits exhibiting a stubborn, self-satisfied ignorance of issues long since raised but also successfully repressed by the positivist, empirically oriented mind-set.

4.9. How are human rights important in the Digital Age? For instance when it comes to that often debated question of security vs. privacy? How might ubiquitous surveillance, or worse still Überveillance, infringe on our freedoms? Crucially, why is privacy important?

Human rights are a Western conception arising within the struggle to assert the power of the secular individual against the ecclesiastic power of the medieval age. In their classical Lockean formulation, human rights consist in the rights of life, liberty and private property. Liberty I take to mean the freedom of movement within three-dimensional time, to cast one's own life in fair power interplay with others. Private property is the core bourgeois right essential to society based on a capitalist economy in which the gainful game is played. The privacy of property consists in an individual's socially acknowledged power to deprive others' access to his or her own property. As such a socially acknowledged power of exclusive possession and use guaranteed by the law of government, it is an individual right. Rights enshrine powers as socially acknowledged and guaranteed, and such powers are exercised by an individual leading his or her life in interplay with others. The exclusivity or privation essential to private property also cuts loose other traditional, hierarchical social and political ties of the individual who then is able to sociate with others via the interplay mediated by thingified value (money). Thus the freedom of association is enhanced. This cutting loose gives rise also to the illusion of the free individual released from any social ties at all. Hence bourgeois individualism. Thingified value as medium of sociation lies hidden beneath the surface appearance of private property of all kinds, i.e. thingified value is the beingness of private property that must be brought to light by a socio-ontological investigation. Thingified value represents the essential socio-ontological condition of possibility of the modern bourgeois individual as such with its characteristic freedoms of movement within society, enabling and empowering it, albeit mediated by thingified power interplays, to shape its own life with others of its choice.

The gamut of individual rights has expanded greatly over the centuries, most notably through rights to be cared for by the state, which has thereby become the modern welfare state. The extension of individual rights to positive rights to be taken care of also renders the individual dependent on this welfare state which thereby, in turn, has the lawful right to pry into individual's private affairs to assess whether the individual concerned is indeed entitled to state welfare support. The supposedly free individual thus becomes the welfare state's dependent client. This is one of the main sources of surveillance encroaching on and restricting privacy in modern societies, today aided and abetted by digital algorithms deployed by the state. Such digitized surveillance of private individuals is complemented by that undertaken by capitalist corporations to further their commercial interests in selling stuff to consumers.

Rights to privacy, on the other side, guarantee that the individual is lawfully empowered to deprive others, especially the state, insight into his or her own affairs, especially financial affairs (in the medium of thingified value). There is a constant tension between the rightful power of the individual to maintain privacy and the state's power to pry into the private individual's life for the sake of raising taxes. The very existence of the state depends on its power to impose taxation on its populace, and such imposition has historically been the spur for struggles, including even revolution. Taxation remains silently and perpetually a vexed issue in societies purportedly based on individual freedom and democracy, and there is invariably an element of arbitrariness in the state's imposition of taxation. Privacy is thus in a tension with and in danger of being undermined by the very instance of power that is supposed to guarantee and defend it. Such a contradiction underlies the movement of continual political struggle between society and state to ward off state incursions into privacy for the sake of raising taxes, but also purportedly for 'our own security' that, more often than not, turns out to be the state's own security.

With the advent of the cyberworld, the individual gains a digitized representation of itself and inevitably leaves behind a digital trace chronicling all its life-movements that greatly enhances the possibilities for deploying algorithms to infiltrate individual privacy and thus undermine the social freedom of movement of an individual leading its own life. In particular, those individuals, such as journalists and activists, involved politically in uncovering and criticizing the state's and the government's actions and misdeeds are in jeopardy of having their privacy eroded and undermined, or even of being imprisoned or killed.

Privacy consists at core in the power to remain hidden to others and is hence an aspect of individual freedom itself in protecting how one leads one's own life free from interference or disparagement. This power becomes a right to privacy when it is socially acknowledged and upheld legally by the state which, in turn, may be constrained by supranational conventions, treaties and laws. Since all rights are socially acknowledged powers, they are themselves subject to ongoing social and political power struggles, i.e. to flux, including the continual danger of their being eroded and rolled back in renewed struggles after having been established through long struggles. Defending privacy is part of the never-ending struggle to defend core rights of individual liberty.

4.10. Should there be any limits to what we can or cannot do in a laboratory in the name of science? Are all options on the table?

The question of should arises along with the question of can, i.e. a question of power. Modern science is all about promoting, furthering the absolute will to effective power over all kinds of movements, both natural and social, thus expanding the ambit of what it can do. This will to power is invariably in league with the striving for gain. The question of should then inevitably arises in response to these expanded can-dos of science, leading to power struggles over what should and should not be allowed in the name of scientific progress in the mastery of movement. At the centre of such social and political struggles are questions relating to what is beneficial or harmful for individuals, for communities, for societies, for our human living on Earth with all its living organisms.

In this sense, ethical questions are not obsolete but, as responsive to a situation, inevitably come too late. They involve the customary practices in which we habitually live our lives. Good ethics are constituted by good life habits, the original sense of ethics. At the heart of such ethical considerations lies, however, the socio-ontological core of mutually estimative power interplays among ourselves along with their resonances in how our customs and habits exhibit an appropriate estimation of the world that today is at the mercy of the modern scientific will to power. Esteem for each other and esteem for the Earth in various power interplays go hand in hand, constituting the historically shifting, socio-ontological core of ethics. Such esteem imposes limits on the unbridled will to power over the movement of whats afforded by technoscience. The hubris of technoscientific mastery is muted to a humility and the modesty of letting nature be what, or even who, it is of itself. Personifying the Earth as Gaia, the name of an ancient god, is a way of freeing the Earth from being conceived merely as a thing for gainful exploitation.

4.11. Will a machine ever be able to love or to experience compassion? Will there ever be algorithms for these expressions?

As already noted, even the concept of consciousness is one of reflective co-knowing of an internal self within the subject; there is an essential doubling of consciousness into consciousness and self-consciousness which could be seen as kind of self-contained egoistic self. In a more adequate conception of human being as psyche in the world, or rather conversely: world in a shared psyche, the self's selfhood is a reflection from the world, offering existential possibilities for self-casting within the openness of three-dimensional time. Such reflections are first and foremost those from others you encounter inevitably in mutually estimative interplays.

This is where phenomena of love and compassion are to be situated socio-ontologically, along with their negations in hate and hard-heartedness, for all of these phenomena are kinds of estimation. Likewise, trust is a feature of the mutuality of interplay; we have to trust *each other*. Compassion is roused when it is seen — or rather, empathetically felt — that someone's personal powers are unable to support their existence adequately in the given situation of the rivalrous power interplay of life. I can feel compassion for someone else because I am a self who is reflective of myself, not merely immersed in myself without difference. As a self I cast who I am from the existential possibilities reflected from the world (perhaps from someone I emulate as a model) and therefore am not simply identical with the masks of selfhood I adopt, but am malleable. Thus I am able also to put myself in someone else's situation and imagine what it is like, the power of imagination being at the core of the psyche. For the most part, our interplay with each other is borne and enabled by trust and mutuality, rather than any kind of self-sacrificing altruism that can be also a mask for dominating the other, for taking care of them in a pejorative sense.

It is not hard to see that algorithmically controlled machines are not capable of such mutually estimative interplay. For a start, machines do not and cannot exist in the three-dimensional temporal openness at all. They are not 'psychic' in this sense and do not shape their selves in an interplay with existential possibilities reflected from the world of others. Lacking selves, they cannot esteem each other in interplay, but at most *react* to each other via reciprocal causality. Hence they are unable to estimate the existential situation of another, i.e. as a self to put one's self empathetically into another's situation.

4.12. What do you see as the three most immediate threats in our 'technological society' that require our urgent attention?

I see as the first urgent threat today the further obliteration of the difference between whatness and whoness being practised above all by neuroscience. To my mind, neuroscience represents the ultimate attack on human being itself by practising the reduction of human being itself, namely, the psyche and the mind, to material, neuronal brain functions that are metaphysically assumed to efficiently cause psychic epiphenomena. This is a most dangerous dogmatic belief nurtured by neuroscience that is being swallowed with scarce resistance by society at large as one of the consequences of the hidden reign of the absolute will to power over movement. There are never-ending genuflections toward neuroscience in the media, i.e. in public opinion, and no self-respecting psychologist can open his or her mouth on an issue without making obeisances to the brain's neuronal workings or its exudation of certain hormones. The equation of the brain with the mind has been long in coming through the centuries, and today has become reigning common sense. One can symptomatically notice the progressive assimilation of whoness into whatness in perverse expressions of everyday language in which the brain itself is addressed or understood as a who, e.g. when it is said that 'the brain thinks this or that...'.

The second increasing danger I see today is the rapid encroachment of the cyberworld on the physical world in which we lived hitherto, with the consequence that more and more of our life-movements are being enabled or hindered by algorithms that outsource our understanding of certain segments of movements in the world, enabling them to be automatically controlled. The substitution of automated algorithmic control for certain mandual or mental tasks results in a progressive disesteeming of employees' skills. There is no 'freedom of choice' in this development. The complacent belief and practice that this algorithmic control is for our own convenience and the betterment of human living, including our security, is self-delusion furthered by modern scientific belief and the powers that be.

Your concept of Überveillance[5] as the embedding of algorithmically controlled, AI-enhanced devices into the human body itself formulates perhaps the ultimate, palpable stage of the cyberworld's incursion into the physical world, with the human body itself thus becoming the most intimate site for surveillance and control of life-movements. Such embedding only makes sense for a way of thinking that is oblivious to the ontological distinction between whatness and whoness. My body is the site of my self, whereas my body conceived as corpus is a physical thing exposed to all sorts of technoscientific manipulation. With such a development, the mutually estimative power interplay among human beings is technologically side-stepped altogether in favour of direct, efficiently productive control for the sake of those who are then in control, with scant protection against their designs.

The third exponentiating danger I see is the state's appropriation of algorithmic control via the cyberworld to keep tabs on and forcefully exert power over its resident population. Even in our supposedly liberal, democratic Western countries, the steady erosion of freedoms of privacy through surveillance and control, under cover of legislation whose legitimation is supposed to reside in enhancing 'our' security, amounts to a cover-up for a gradual slide into totalitarian state control. In my view, the increasing deployment of algorithms by the state to enforce its raising of taxes is an underestimated danger whose underestimation goes hand in hand with the (socio-ontological) idea that the (paternalistic welfare) state exercises its technocratic power to effect the socially just redistribution of produced wealth. Taxation is also regarded as a steering mechanism for steering the behaviour of the state's consumer-denizens, nudging and forcing them to move in a certain direction. Seen in this way, taxation becomes a kind of adjusting screw for adjusting the movements of a complicated machine called society. Such technocratic ways of thinking are rife today, including among ostensibly progressive political forces such as the environmental movement.

---

5 Cf. *Uberveillance and the Social Implications of Microchip Implants: Emerging Technologies* M.G.Michael and Katina Michael, IGI Global: USA, 2014.

4.13. The designers, builders and operators of these new technologies: to whom are they accountable? What is accountability in this context? Must these groups grapple with moral questions?

The proponents, initiators and implementers of digital technologies are mostly accountable only within the companies they work for, and that primarily with respect to profitability, that is, the striving for gain. They and their companies can only be made accountable by the wider discourse of civil society on how these technologies potentially or actually reshape our customary way of life with one another, either beneficially or detrimentally. These are not moral questions — which concern individual conscience — but social and political issues that are inevitably controversial because they impinge on how we are able to live and what we value in our lives. Our sociating interplay is very often controversial, especially because the truth of contestable issues regarding digital technologies is invariably ambiguous. Such ambiguity can only be resolved in controversy that brings the state of affairs to light, as a prelude to making a social decision about the pros and cons of a given technology. Underlying such debates are questions relating to how we are to live in customary practices with one another that are never finally resolved but perhaps decided for a time by political majorities rather than unanimously, i.e. by a united soul. In this way, companies developing and implementing such technologies are called to account. The social and political struggle over the appropriate employment of digital technologies can also be fought out via the medium of thingified value insofar as the members of civil society are themselves investors who save during their working lives for retirement. Pension funds (superannuation funds) therefore can exert pressure on the activities of capitalist enterprises through their investment policies that can include evaluations of the harmfulness or otherwise of digital technologies.

Harmony and concord in social and political interplay, which is essentially always power interplay, is mostly short-lived. The movement of society is driven by contradictions between opposing forces in interplay (not just interaction) with one another. The unified soul of an age we all ineluctably share in the attunement and mind-set of the time is nevertheless splintered and fragmented into many individual perspectives including, in particular, each individual player's position and prospects in the gainful game that result inevitably in opposed interests. Our historical mind-set is beholden to the two gods I have mentioned, Willy P. and Pleon Exia, who keep our mind in thrall and remain invisible for as long as we are trapped in the metaphysical illusion of our own underlying subjectivity. In this sense, to ask to whom the originators of new digital technologies are accountable presumes a subjectivity that has already been surrendered to today's cyberworld that is a consummate realization of the absolute will to power over movement. This has a parallel with the gainful game played in the medium of thingified value when, for instance, a capitalist enterprise is forced by the conditions of competition to sack thousands of workers because, ultimately, the enterprise itself is merely a player playing according to the rules of augmentation of reified value, and is thus not an underlying, responsible subject. In this situation, ultimately there is an historical responsibility to learn to think ontologically to see how our mind-set has been cast historically in order to gain distance from it. Such insight can serve as an important orienting backdrop for ongoing socio-political struggles over new digital technologies.

4.14. Some 'innovators' want to do away with the flesh in their quest to fuse us with the machine. Are they after immortality? What is 'good' or 'bad' with this quest? Are there some dangerous implications?

Such innovators certainly seem to be after immortality, a misguided quest insofar as immortality is not a matter of the never-ending prolongation of the life of a fleshly body, but of the lastingness of how you continue to be esteemed in the shared openness of three-dimensional, historical time. Their ambitions aim unknowingly at the supercession of human being itself in an ontological sense, i.e. in its beingness, which I propose has to be conceived clearly as whoness in contradistinction to ubiquitous whatness. Human being is fleshly in the sense that I, as a self, have my own body that is irreducible to a merely physical corpus. Through my body I continually occupy places in the world among extended physical things that are also located in their respective places from which I take my orientation. The 'innovators' are blithe proponents of the absorption of whoness into whatness who skip over questions such as what it means for you or me to exist bodily in certain places rather than as things assuming certain positions in abstract space of which they themselves are unaware, since they are not self-reflective of the world with its existential possibilities.

Could a disembodied, silicon-based consciousness be a self? Since all consciousness is necessarily a co-knowing (con-scientia) consciousness of itself, and this self can only cast itself from reflections from and projections into three-dimensional time (who was I, who am I and who will I become?), it is hardly plausible that any kind of machine in its whatness could be exposed to such existential 3D-time of which it cannot be aware. Human being itself is characterized essentially by both understanding and moodedness. As mooded it is attuned with the world embedded in 3D-time, and such mooded attunement includes a bodily resonance with the world that shows itself in emotions of all kinds — joy, sadness, grief, contentment, rage, etc. My body participates movingly in my moodedness in any given situation through its emotions. Extreme moods of elation and distress, for instance, show themselves clearly in the emotionally resonating body.

This is perhaps the ontological end-game being played out today, whether we learn to see who we are in truth instead of being trapped (unknowingly, cluelessly) in the ontology of whatness and thus blind to whoness that enables beings to present themselves in another light, another guise, *other*wise. Such truth is not a matter of logical argumentation to bolster and defend a 'position', as it has been for millennia, remaining thus today in academic philosophical discourse, but of disclosing elementary phenomena of human being itself in their simplicity, at whose core is the phenomenon of mutually estimative interplay. What is 'bad' in the quest of these technological 'innovators' is their wilful blindness to an alternative way of looking at the world, that is, basically, to an alternative ontology. Such wilful blindness stems from a smug technoscientific hubris suffering from tunnel vision. Mainstream philosophy, in turn, has long since accommodated itself to its diminished status as handmaiden and whore to modern technoscience, assigned a supporting role for technoscience in its never-ending striving for enhanced mastery over movement of all kinds. This has already resulted in an ontological impoverishment for the mind.

In particular, analytic philosophy covers modern science's back by suppressing genuine ontological questions as situated beyond the pale in metaphysics which it regards as superseded. At most, mainstream philosophy has ethical misgivings, whilst being unable to see that all questions of ethics are grounded in the social movement of estimative power interplays over the customs in which live in an historical time. This mainstream philosophy, more recently, does include a discipline it calls ontology, but it is an ontology that investigates only 'what exists' (and not the question as to the meaning of being itself) and is oblivious to the *ontological difference* through which beings are cast hermeneutically AS the beings they are. This hermeneutic AS is historically malleable and can be recast in the openness of historical 3D-time to encompass also an ontology of whoness. Today's academic philosophy is entrusted by the absolute will to power over movement with the crucial task of keeping the lid on the ontological difference tightly closed.

Biographical Note

Michael Eldred

Michael Eldred was born in 1952 in Katoomba and grew up in Leura and Katoomba in the Blue Mountains close to Sydney. He started studies in 1970 at the University of Sydney, first completing two science degrees majoring in mathematics, but including one year of philosophy. In 1975 he returned to philosophy, experiencing in 1976, through a visiting lecturer from Constance named Volkbert 'Mike' Roth, his introduction to the then-current, ongoing German discussion aiming at a critical reassessment and reconstruction of Marx's encompassing project of a theory of bourgeois society. The debate had been triggered by Hans-Georg Backhaus, one of Adorno's students, by a seminar paper Backhaus delivered in 1965. Marx himself had only ever completed multiple drafts for the first part of his six-part project under the title of *Das Kapital: Kritik der politischen Ökonomie*. He left behind not even completed drafts of his original plans for a comprehensive theory of the bourgeois 'superstructure'. Eldred was awarded his PhD by the General Philosophy Department at Sydney University in 1984 with a dissertation on the reconstruction and extension of a form-analytic theory of capitalist society in a critical engagement especially with Marx and Hegel. Eldred was a tutor in both pure mathematics and philosophy at Sydney University and has taught courses at Constance University, the Pädagogische Hochschule in Munich, Witten-Herdecke University and for the Daseinsanalytische Gesellschaft in Zürich.

By translating Peter Sloterdijk's *Critique of Cynical Reason* in 1984 for Minnesota U.P., he came across Heidegger's *Being and Time* and phenomenology of the Heideggerian kind. This provided the impulse for intensive study of Heidegger's writings that led him to the Greeks, especially Plato and Aristotle. Heidegger's earlier lectures opened his eyes to how to read these seminal Western thinkers anew phenomenologically. Already at this time in the mid-1980s, he started a project on the question of whoness (a concept from *Being and Time*) in relation to an ontological gender difference between masculinity and femininity that resulted in two published books on masculine whoness in German. The interest in gender difference was a legacy of his time in General Philosophy, where feminism in the 1970s was a strong influence. By the early 2000s, the questioning of whoness had transformed into a wider socio-ontological inquiry, including questions of values as well as social and political power, and culminating in his *Social Ontology of Whoness: Rethinking core phenomena of political philosophy* (2019).

One of the major impulses for Eldred's work has been to uncover the respective, quasi complementary, blind spots in Marx's and Heidegger's thinking, first published in 2000 in German and then in various editions, most recently in 2015, under the title *Capital and Technology: Marx and Heidegger*.

In 1990 he met the philosopher, Rafael Capurro, with whom he had e-mail correspondence in 1999 that developed the first scant outlines of a digital ontology. This intial exchange bore fruit as several articles and books by Eldred, most recently in his *Movement and Time in the Cyberworld: Questioning the Digital Cast of Being* (2019).

Eldred earned his livelihood from 1985 on as a freelance translator, gradually becoming specialized in contemporary-art catalogues. This occupation had the side-benefit of maintaining his independence from the rules of play in academic institutions and leaving him time for philosophical work.

He started playing guitar at the age of ten, which has accompanied him throughout his life. In recent years he has recorded several of his own philosophical songs (philorock) on a non-commercial basis and has also published a book on the phenomenology of music.

From a first marriage he has a daughter, Rachel Eldred, who lives in Sydney, and from a fateful encounter at a conference in Hamburg under the title *Eros, Liebe, Sexus* at the end of Septermber 1990, he has a philosopher-wife, Astrid Nettling, with whom he lives in Cologne.

Selected Books and Articles by Michael Eldred

Critique of Competitive Freedom and the Bourgeois-Democratic State: Outline of a Form-Analytic Extension of Marx's Uncompleted System with an Appendix *A Value-Form Analytic Reconstruction of 'Capital'* co-authored with M. Hanlon, L. Kleiber & M. Roth, Kurasje, Copenhagen 1984 (republished in an emended edition with CreateSpace, North Charleston 2015).

Capital and Technology: Marx and Heidegger first published in *Left Curve* No. 24, May 2000 (translated into Chinese; originally published in German. A thoroughly revised edition is available from CreateSpace, North Charleston 2015).

Social Ontology: Recasting Political Philosophy Through a Phenomenology of Whoness ontos verlag, Frankfurt 2008.

Social Ontology of Whoness: Rethinking Core Phenomena of Political Philosophy third emended, revised and expanded edition of the preceding, De Gruyter, Berlin 2019a.

The Digital Cast of Being: Metaphysics, Mathematics, Cartesianism, Cybernetics, Capitalism, Communication ontos verlag, Frankfurt 2009.

Movement and Time in the Cyberworld: Questioning the Digital Cast of Being De Gruyter, Berlin 2019b (revised and expanded version of the preceding).

The Land of Matta: A philosophical, quantum-mechanical phantasy CreateSpace, North Charleston 2015.

'Turing's cyberworld of timelessly copulating bit-strings' www.arte-fact.org 2012. Abridged version published under the title 'Turing's Cyberworld' in *Information Cultures in the Digital Age: A Festschrift in Honour of Rafael Capurro* Matthew Kelly & Jared Bielby (eds.) Springer VS, Wiesbaden 2016 pp. 65-81.

'Technology, Technique, Interplay: Questioning Die Frage nach der Technik' June 2006 at artefact. Paper first presented to the conference *4. Aussprache über die Philosophie Martin Heideggers* 01-03 June 2006 at the Bergische University in Wuppertal, Germany, convened by Peter Trawny and Eric S. Nelson. Presented also to the School of Philosophy at the University of Sydney on 10 September 2008 at the invitation of Duncan Ivison, and to the 41st Annual North American Heidegger Conference 03-05 May 2007 at DePaul University in Chicago, convened by Sean D. Kirkland, Will McNeill & Maureen

Melnyk. Published in the Proceedings of the 41st North American Heidegger Conference DePaul University, Chicago 3-5 May 2007.

'Technology, Technique, Interplay: Questioning Die Frage nach der Technik' *Technology and Society Magazine* IEEE Issue 2, Summer 2013 pp. 13-21, slightly abridged version of the preceding.

Digital Whoness: Identity, Privacy and Freedom in the Cyberworld (with Rafael Capurro & Daniel Nagel) ontos/de Gruyter, Frankfurt 2013.

A Question of Time: An alternative cast of mind CreateSpace, North Charleston 2015.

Thinking of Music: An approach along a parallel path CreateSpace, North Charleston 2015.

Heidegger, Hölderlin e John Cage translated and with a postface by Agostino Di Scipio, Semar Publishers, Rome 2000.

Der Mann: Geschlechterontologischer Auslegungsversuch der phallologischen Ständigkeit Haag + Herchen, Frankfurt 1989.

Phänomenologie der Männlichkeit: kaum ständig noch Verlag Dr. Josef H. Röll, Dettelbach 1999.

Entständigung: Philosophische Aufsätze CreateSpace, North Charleston 2015.

A more extensive list of publications is available at www.arte-fact.org. These include:
'11 Thesen zum heutigen digitalen Entwurf des Seins' 1996
'Anglophone Justice Theory, the Gainful Game and the Political Power Play' 2009, revised version in Eldred 2019a.
'Assessing How Heidegger Thinks Power Through the History of Being' 2004
'Digital Being, the Real Continuum, the Rational and the Irrational' 2010
'The Principle of Reason and Justice' 2006, revised version in Eldred 2019a.
'Absolutely Divine Everyday: Tracing Heidegger's thinking on godliness' With an appendix on 'Aristotle's purely energetic god of the fair' 2008/2020.

Numerous blog posts at artefactphil.arte-fact.org are also pertinent, including:
Cyberworld and cybersecurity 18 February 2021
Modern physics built on quicksand? 23 December 2020

Contradictions in time 10 July 2016
Aristotle deleted 07 June 2016
Science doesn't think 07 June 2016
Rechte / Rights 20 January 2016
Meaningful presence 21 September 2015
Feminist Metaphysics 04 August 2015
Modern scholasticism 21 July 2015
Academia's Geistesgestell 18 July 2015
Sociology: philosophy democratized 21 February 2015
Superseded paradigm subjectivity 14 January 2015
Why modern science stays dumb 08 January 2015
Essence of truth as effectiveness, and 3D-time 21 September 2014
Electron Liberation Movement 17 September 2014
Science's value-freedom bogus 22 August 2014
Presencing, absencing, disclosing, hiding 24 June 2014
Set-up vs. gainful game 11 June 2014
Interplay of free starting-points in the time-clearing 31 May 2014
Singularity cannot be con-cluded 30 May 2014
Negative and positive freedom 23 April 2014
Science and scholarship don't think 19 April 2014
Continuum and Time: Weyl after Heidegger 24 March 2014
Elimination of time 19 March 2014
Subject loses control, turns cannibal 10 February 2014
Letting presence and letting presents presence 04 February 2014
Dasein and the time-clearing 28 January 2014
Darwinian evolution's teleology 24 January 2014
Parmenides' message 12 December 2013
Task of Philosophy 05 August 2013
Human body a used vehicle 02 August 2013
Modern science's impoverished metaphysics 30 May 2013
Hiatus singularity/universality 03 March 2013
Commutative and distributive justice 22 February 2013
Fission impossible. Fusion accomplished 08 August 2012
Higgs' boson or subject-object split? 10 July 2012
Totalizing, megalomanic modern science 28 June 2012
Potentiality and Actuality 22 June 2012
Humanism's roots in modern subjectivist metaphysics 19 May 2012

Index

N

O

T

www.ingramcontent.com/pod-product-compliance
Ingram Content Group UK Ltd.
Pitfield, Milton Keynes, MK11 3LW, UK
UKHW020136250726
13967UKWH00002B/679

9 781741 283389